EUARE 1

EUARE LECTURES
EX NIHILO AND FIRST ANNUAL CONFERENCE
2017–2018

Edited by Francesca Cadeddu

EuARe Executive Board: Karla Boersma, Francesca Cadeddu, Jocelyne Cesari, Silvio Ferrari, Vincente Fortier, Hans-Peter Grosshans, Pantelis Kalaitzidis, Frederik Pedersen, Herman Selderhuis

EUROPEAN ACADEMY OF RELIGION

EUARE LECTURES
Francesca Cadeddu, Series Editor

Graphic Design Project   Cristina Barone
www.europeanacademyofreligion.org

in cooperation with

Opera realizzata con il supporto di Regione Emilia-Romagna

First Edition 2019
ISBN 978-88-96118-07-8

© 2019 by Fondazione per le scienze religiose Giovanni XXIII
via San Vitale 114
40125 Bologna

All rights reserved. No part of this work – text and images – may be reproduced or utilezed in any form or by any means, electronic or mechanical, including photocopying, recording, or any information storage and retrieval system, without prior written permission from the publisher.

Contents

7   Introduction ~ Francesca Cadeddu

15   The Hebrew Names of Jesus in Renaissance Christian Kabbalah ~ Saverio Campanini

49   A Productive Coexistence for Theology and Religious Studies. What Kind of Work is Needed on Both Sides? ~ Pierre Gisel
- 49   1. A Proposal
- 50   2. A Contentious Background
- 54   3. Theologising Once Again Correlated to Particularity and Subjected to Critical Trial
- 58   4. For a Genealogical Approach to the Questions Related to Defining the Issues
- 61   5. For a Productive Coexistence of Theology and Religious Studies

71   The Changing Soul of Europe: The Challenge to the Secular State ~ Enzo Pace
- 71   1. Introduction
- 75   2. Visible Religious Diversity: Gurudwara, Mandir, Mosques, Orthodox Parishes, Buddhist Pagodas, Neo-Pentecostal African Churches
- 80   3. The Growing SBNR (Spiritual But Not Religious People)
- 84   4. Conclusion

87   Mutual Recognition in Theology and Modern Society ~ Risto Saarinen
- 87   1. Current Politics of Recognition
- 91   2. Recognition and Religion: Ancient Roots
- 95   3. Medieval and Early Modern Recognition Discourses
- 102   4. Religious Recognition in Modernity
- 111   5. Recognition in Ecumenical Theology: Difference and Equality

- 117 Methodological Principles: Luther, the Representative of a "World We Have Lost" ~ Heinz Schilling
  - 119 1. New Principles in Commemorating Luther and the Reformation
  - 121 2. A Faith That Is of the World
  - 124 3. State and Politics
  - 128 4. Christians and Jews
  - 129 4.1 The Historical Facts
  - 134 4.2 Long Term Impact
  - 136 5. Freedom of Conscience and Its Pre-Modern Meaning
  - 138 6. The Impact on Catholicism
  - 142 7. The End of Universalism and the Rise of Modern Differentiation in European Religion and Culture
- 147 A Fractal Interpretation of Religious Diversity ~ Perry Schmidt-Leukel
  - 148 1. Fractals in Inorganic and Organic Nature
  - 156 2. Fractal Structures in Culture and Religion
  - 167 3. Interreligious Theology and the Fractal View of Religious Diversity
  - 173 4. The Fruitfulness of the Theory
- 179 The Controversial Image of Moses in Rabbinic Literature ~ Lieve Teugels
- 191 Martin Luther, the Eleutherius: The Freedom of Intended Ambiguity of Theology and Gender ~ Else Marie Wiberg Pedersen
  - 191 1. Introduction
  - 195 2. Sola Scriptura, Translation, and Gender
  - 199 3. Women and Luther's Theology
  - 199 4. Women in the Bible
  - 206 5. Gender and Church
- 221 Notes on Contributors
- 229 Names Index

Introduction
Francesca Cadeddu

The European Academy of Religion (EuARe) is a research initiative, launched under the patronage of the European Parliament, which offers an exchange platform to the variety of academic institutions, journals, publishers, media and scholars in Europe and the surrounding regions. In 2015, the research team of the Fondazione per le scienze religiose (Fscire) realised that, given the role that religion plays in the lives of most Europeans and the religious diversity of our society, both individual scholars and academic, political and cultural institutions should transform their knowledge into a highly powerful tool to be used against religious illiteracy, in favour of peaceful coexistence and diversity acceptance.

Therefore, thanks to the impulse of Alberto Melloni, Secretary of Fscire and main promoter of the initiative, and also to the support of hundreds of scholars and the European Commission, Fscire has been able to set up a database of contacts of scholarly associations, scientific societies, research centres, university departments, working groups and a plurality of other organisations engaged in the study of religions. Over 1,800 institutions were initially surveyed and they confirmed the extent of the field of religious studies and the need to provide this 'archipelago' with a common platform. This need has become all the more pressing now that the debate on religions poses key challenges to our societies, in terms of freedom and rights.

In the summer of 2016, approximately 3,000 invitations to convene in Bologna were sent to the institutions and scholars surveyed, and the positive response has been overwhelming: on December 5, 2016, at the founding event of the European Academy of Religion, Fscire hosted more than 500 participants (both institutions and individuals coming from all over Europe, the MENA countries, Caucasus, Russia, America and Asia) along with 25 universities that agreed to act as mentors of the Academy in conjunction with the Universities of Bologna, Oxford and Paris, which have been active supporters of the initiative from the outset.

The event opened with keynote speeches by the EU Commissioner, Carlos Moedas, and by other distinguished academics, diplomats and representatives of OSCE/ODIHR, UNESCO and the World Economic Forum. In the afternoon, researchers and scholars worked together in three parallel sessions in order to define a statute for the Academy, organise the first annual meeting and submit proposals and ideas for the research platform. The proposals and suggestions made within the three discussion groups were collected and examined by the moderators of each committee. Together with the organisational secretariat, moderators constituted the international board of the newly-formed association.

The day was an opportunity for everyone to meet, discuss and raise awareness about the institutions to which they are affiliated. In order to foster mutual understanding and encourage dialogue, a catalogue describing all the parties involved was distributed on the day of the event.

The project has also gained the attention of Italian and European institutions, receiving the High Patronage of the European Parliament, the Patronage of the Italian Ministry of Education, University and Research as well as the Italian Ministry of Foreign Affairs and International Cooperation. They have all continued to work with Fscire in the past years, and it is a common aim to strengthen these relationships as the association grows and develops.

Such an approach lies in the very nature of the EuARe: it wishes to provide a common voice to all the disciplines holding an academic status in universities or research centres, while enabling them to express their own specific, distinctive epistemological traditions. This is the reason why EuARe promotes academic and interdisciplinary exchange, mutual respect among individuals and communities of a diverse religion or belief and provides a real, open space to those who work in the production and/or dissemination of knowledge in, and of, the religious field. EuARe chose to be as inclusive as possible, hence it is also connected to groups external to academia, in order to create understanding in the public domain concerning developments that involve religious aspects or motivations, encourage stakeholders in Europe to address the post-secular resurgence of the role of religion in the public sphere and contribute to the construction of society and the formation of culture.

EuARe's enthusiasm was shared by our associates at the very beginning, and, therefore, the provisional international executive board decided to explore the possibility of organising a second meeting in 2017 (a Zero Conference, waiting for the First Annual Conference in 2018), having the primary objective of testing its capacity to be an inclusive platform for exchange and cooperation.

The conference program was therefore structured in order to permit the affiliated institutions to present studies and ongoing activities. It took place under the auspices of the G7 Italian Presidency and was organised in collaboration with the Italian Ministry of Education, University and Research. It was opened by the addresses, among others, of the Special Envoy for Freedom of Religion or Belief outside the EU, Ján Figel', and the Rector of the University of Bologna, Francesco Ubertini. During the five-day conference there were 133 panels, constituting a total of 568 interventions and involving 950 participants.

The First Annual Conference, held in the first week of March 2018, was equally successful: about a thousand participants came from all over Europe, from Russia, Caucasus, the Balkans, Georgia, Ukraine, Israel, Sudan, Korea, Pakistan, Malaysia, Chile, Colombia, China, India and many other countries.

On that occasion, EuARe established some fruitful partnerships, among others with ISPI, the Italian Institute for International Political Studies, which is based in Milan and which organised its annual International Workshop on Religion and International Relations and a Public Roundtable on Interreligious Dialogue and Foreign Policy within the conference. As a part of the partnership, they also kindly hosted the EuARe at the fourth edition of the Rome

MED Dialogues, a high-level annual initiative promoted by the Italian Ministry of Foreign Affairs and International Cooperation and by ISPI in Rome. EuARe took part in the Pre-MED Dialogues with a religion forum entitled "Religion and International Relations: Setting a Mediterranean Agenda", with guests from Italy, the United Kingdom, Jordan, the United States, Sudan and Saudi Arabia.

Other promising partnerships include the International Consortium for Law and Religion Studies, which supports the organisation of an International Moot Court Competition, and also the European Society for the Philosophy of Religion, the European Network of Buddhist-Christian Studies, the ADEC Association of University professors working on law and religious phenomena, the Italian Association for Philosophy of Religion, the Jagiellonian University in Kraków, master studies in the prevention of the radicalisation of terrorism and politics for interreligious and intercultural integration at the Law Department of the University of Bari, Georgetown University, Link Campus University, Confronti Study Centre, and the Centre for the Study of Religion and Politics of the University of St Andrews. Since then, many ohther academic and non-academic institutions became part if the EuARe's platform.

Finally, the Emilia-Romagna Region, together with the Fscire, established the Giuseppe Alberigo Award, which offers 20,000 euros to an established scholar and 10,000 to one in the early years of his or her career. Alberigo dedicated 54 years' work to the Fscire, and the award is assigned in memory of his passion and critical contribution.

Francesca Cadeddu

The programme of each of these initiatives well reflects EuARe's approach, choices and inclusiveness. EuARe is constantly working to involve all academic disciplines and European countries, while establishing ties with scholars from nearby regions and other continents. Such a variety of disciplinary, methodological and geographical approaches was and will be clearly reflected in the many lectures and roundtables hosted by EuARe, and this volume is the first in a series whose aim is to keep track of the topics and changes which guide research, understanding and dissemination within the many disciplines involved in the study of religion in Europe. In the following pages you will find some of the lectures delivered at the Ex Nihilo Zero Conference and the First Annual Conference, while the following issues will be dedicated to one annual conference each. Here you will read the lectures held by Saverio Campanini (University of Bologna), Pierre Gisel (University of Lausanne), Enzo Pace (University of Padova), Else Marie Wiberg Pedersen (Aarhus University), Risto Saarinen (University of Helsinki), Heinz Schilling (Emeritus, Humboldt University of Berlin), Perry Schmidt-Leukel (University of Münster) and Lieve Teugels (Utrecht University). Each author is a leading European scholar within his or her own field of expertise and will guide us through the themes which set the pace of recent scholarly debates. The heterogeneity of the topics is precisely the distinctive mark of EuARe: we support the disciplinary and interdisciplinary creation and dissemination of knowledge in order to contribute to the construction of society and the formation of culture.

EUARE LECTURES

The Hebrew Names of Jesus in Renaissance Christian Kabbalah
Saverio Campanini

> *Si quid trecenti bis novenis additis*
> *possint, figura noverimus mystica.*
> Prudentius

If one considers the central role of the name of Jesus within the theological field of Christianity, one might imagine that from antiquity Christians could have reached some kind of consensus concerning the pronunciation and the correct form of this name in the original language in which Jesus was named at birth, and which was certainly used to call him and to evoke his power in operating miracles. Although in extensively Hellenised Palestine at the end of the first century, before the Common Age, the use of Greek names was very widespread, unlike the parents of the Apostle Philip, to give just one example, Jesus' parents did not recur to purely Greek onomastics to name their child. If one looks at the question more closely, however, the situation appears much more complex: nobody, either during the patristic age, in the Middle Ages or in the Renaissance, could state that s/he was absolutely certain about the etymology of Jesus' name. One cannot dismiss the problem by stating, however tempting this might appear, that the Christians were simply not interested in the question because one can find some scattered mentions of the name of Jesus in Hebrew (usually in transcriptions, but also, at times, as we shall see, in the original script); yet the various forms suggested do not coincide. In other words, there are different versions of the name, even if this fact is not considered perturbing.

The attempts, found in the works of some medieval authors, usually following the *Etymologies* of Isidore of Sevilla, to spell the true name of Jesus, more often than not in transcription, amounted mainly to a mere curiosity without any significant theological bearing. In general, one can safely assume that Hebrew among the Christians had not only been forgotten but that even the awareness of the importance of Hebrew had been lost. At the same time, Hebrew did not vanish either in antiquity or in the Middle Ages, and it did not become an exotic language to be found in some remote region, far beyond geographical and political boundaries. This presents a rather interesting paradox, which often resurfaced in matters concerning Hebrew and the Jews among the Christians. As a matter of fact, Jews and Hebrew books were found far more frequently in Europe during the Middle Ages than in the Renaissance (that is to say, in the age of the re-discovery of Hebrew by Christians). One might even raise the question as to whether the Christian interest in Hebrew was not directly related to the expulsion of the Jews from the majority of European countries between the end of the Middle Ages and the beginning of the Renaissance.

The Hebrew Names of Jesus in Renaissance Christian Kabbalah

In the epoch that forms the core of our interest in this context, between the end of the fifteenth and the first half of the sixteenth century, a scholar about whom more will be said, Johannes Reuchlin, revealed a peculiarly acute awareness of the problem. In the preface to his Hebrew grammar (*De rudimentis Hebraicis*), published in 1506, he writes that the expulsion of the Jews from the Iberian Peninsula (and from many towns in the Empire) signified a decisive cultural and theological challenge for Christians. Europe without Jews was for him a catastrophe, not so much in consideration of the predicament and the sufferings of the Jews themselves but because this would mean losing a unique opportunity to learn Hebrew and inquire into Jewish literature before they vanished from sight. Without Hebrew, according to Reuchlin, one cannot understand the meaning of the Christian advent and the revelation it implies completely. Without the Jews, the chance to learn Hebrew became less likely. This lent urgency to the model he proposed, stripping the Jews of their monopolistic ownership of the grammatical tools for learning and even teaching oneself Hebrew, a project for which the Latin grammar and dictionary of Hebrew he was launching would be the perfect platform.

This unprecedented evaluation of the role and the significance of the Hebrew language did not originate in Reuchlin's personal initiative but was rather the continuation of the most accomplished development of Florentine humanism: it was in Florence, where humanism 'invented' the renaissance of Greek in the aftermath of yet another catastrophe, that is to say the fall of Constantinople in

1453, that the young Pico della Mirandola attempted to add the knowledge of Hebrew to the Graeco-Latin canon of the indispensable languages that a philosopher had to master. The audacity of Pico della Mirandola consisted in setting Hebrew on the same plane as Greek and Latin, already imagining *de facto* what would later be described as the trilingual programme of humanism. The end of this story is known: we are aware that the programme foreseen by Pico and his followers was too extensive, or too advanced, for its age, or simply too imprudent, since Pico failed to recognise the danger of suddenly inverting the polarity from the ill-acknowledged language, belonging to a despised religion, culture and ethnicity, to a model of knowledge and the culmination of theology and piety. This radical revision of a traditional image, or prejudice turned away from the received stereotype envisioning Hebrew as a devilish tongue, a superstitious blabbering or, at best, a language suited for desperate magicians, incapable of describing reality and even less of addressing God since the Jews using and praising it failed to recognise Jesus as the Messiah and even less as the Son of God. It is not difficult to criticise the first Hebraists for their lack of 'political' realism, but what is really astounding is that in point of fact the Renaissance Hebraists did have some chances of being successful.

It will not be possible, in this context, to go into detail but it will suffice to note that, starting with Pico della Mirandola himself, the true motor behind this new perspective on Judaism and on the potential of Hebrew as a verification of Christian revelation can be identified in the less known literary and religious genre of Kabbalah. The function of Kabbalah for Pico della Mirandola and his followers was mainly conceived as a method for overcoming the impasses of scholasticism, on the one hand, and of the esthetic paganisation of a merely literary humanism, on the other. The ideal of *Concordia* permitted a synthesis between Platonism and Aristotelianism resembling Ficino's syncretism, but was much less prudent, harbouring the idea of a convergence of religions in a profoundly renewed Christianity. Why Kabbalah? For several reasons, among others because of the exegetical method of gematria, which made it possible to go back to the letter of Revelation and at the same time break down the wall of literalism, injecting by exegetical means a new dynamism into the text of the Scriptures. To mention just one further reason for the preference accorded to Kabbalah: the very concept of emanation, at the core of Kabbalistic speculations, facilitated a conciliation between biblical creationism and Neoplatonic philosophy. Pico observes that in reading the Kabbalists he had the impression not of reading Jewish texts, but Christian authors that were very much in harmony with the church fathers, especially those most influenced by Neoplatonism.

The main topic of the present contribution, however, does not focus on those great theological or philosophical questions but on an apparently minor subject, a detail, that nevertheless is not without importance: the question of the name of Jesus. Even within this fairly limited field, as will clearly emerge, the Christian Kabbalists of the Renaissance did not agree on the issue. This is remarkable for an intellectual movement writing *Concordia* on its banners; nevertheless, this disagreement, which was in many cases more apparent than substantial, deserves, in my opinion, to be analysed and understood rather than dismissed as marginal, irrelevant or too esoteric.

The first Christian Kabbalist, Pico della Mirandola, was also the first scholar to suggest not only a peculiar form of the Hebrew name of Jesus, but also its mystical interpretation. The first edition of his *Conclusiones* (*Theses*), printed in Rome at the end of 1486, does not contain, for technical reasons, any Hebrew characters. Nevertheless, his allusions are sufficiently clear to leave no room for doubt as to his conception of the name. At the same time, they are ambiguous enough to explain that his disciples could construe on their very basis different solutions, until Arcangelo da Borgonovo (or rather, as I shall suggest below, Johannes Reuchlin) arrived at the formulation of a solution of compromise.

The questions that deserve to be addressed here are the following: how Pico came to his name of Jesus, in which terms he described it and why his peculiar form of the name is relevant. The terms he used to speak about the name are strictly related to the literary genre of the *Conclusiones*, promoting brevity and synthesis, even if the space left open to interpretation, partly caused by the technical shortcomings of the first edition, contributed greatly to the divergent claims observable among his followers. One needs, therefore, to focus on the exact formulation he chose.

In the seventh thesis of the series *Secundum opinionem propriam* (that is, to his mind), Pico writes:

The Hebrew Names of Jesus in Renaissance Christian Kabbalah

> No Hebrew Cabalist can deny that the name Jesus, if we interpret it following the method and principles of the Cabala, signifies precisely all this and nothing else, that is: *God the Son of God and the Wisdom of the Father, united to human nature in the unity of assumption through the third Person of God, who is the ardent fire of love.*[1]

A complete explanation of what Pico might have meant by this bold statement would require far more space than permitted by the structure of the present essay. We shall need, therefore, to take his words at face value, since Pico himself did not explain them, because the public discussion he imagined for his propositions did not take place and nobody can be certain of how exactly he would have argued in their defense. However, one question remains: if the result of several Councils and of innumerable theological discussions in the first centuries of Church history were to be contained in a name, how did it sound and how should it be written?

One possible answer to this question can be found in the thesis immediately preceding the one we have just quoted:

---

[1] "Nullus hebraeus cabalista potest negare quod nomen Iesu, si eum secundum modum et principia cabalae interpretemur, hoc totum precise et nihil alius significat, id est, deum dei filium patrisque sapientiam per tertiam divinitatis personam, quae est ardentissimus amoris ignis, naturae humanae in unitate suppositi unitum". Cf. S.A. Farmer, *Syncretism in the West: Pico's 900 Theses (1486). The Evolution of Traditional Religious and Philosophical Systems* (Tempe: Arizona Center for Medieval and Renaissance Studies, 1998), 522–523.

> Whoever is profound in the science of the Cabala can understand that the three great four-letter names of God, which exist in the secrets of the Cabalists, through miraculous appropriation should be attributed to the three Persons of the Trinity like this: so that the name <אהיה Ehyeh> is that of the Father, the name <יהוה YHVH> of the Son, the name <אדני Adonai> of the Holy Spirit.[2]

Pico's words are only apparently less obscure, since even on this point his theory will be the object of reciprocally incompatible interpretations, although I shall not expand on them here. Nevertheless, it seems indisputable that Pico proposes to tie the person of the Son to the Tetragram, that is to say, not only to the Messiah, as Chaim Wirszubski remarked,[3] but also to the Son as such. Now, it is certainly true that Pico affirms in a different passage that, at least according to Kabbalists, the Tetragram was the name of the Messiah, as one reads in the fifteenth conclusion to the same series:

> By the name *Yod he vav he*, which is the ineffable name that the Cabalists say will be the name of the Messiah, it is clearly known that he will be God the Son of God made

---

[2] "Tria magna dei nomina quaternaria, quae sunt in secretis cabalistarum, per mirabilem appropriationem tribus personis trinitatis ita debere attribui, ut nomen אהיה sit patris, nomen יהוה sit filii, nomen אדני sit spiritus sancti, intelligere potest qui in scientia cabalae fuerit profundus". Ibid.

[3] Cf. C. Wirszusbki, *Pico della Mirandola's Encounter with Jewish Mysticism* (Cambridge, Mass.: Harvard University Press, 1989), 218.

man through the Holy Spirit, and that after him the Paraclete will descend over men for the perfection of mankind.[4]

Until recently one did not exactly know how to understand Pico's statement according to which the name of Jesus was to be identified with the Tetragram and why, as we have seen, he related this idea to the persuasion that the Son and the Tetragram were connected, especially since it seemed that no Kabbalistic source could justify this claim.[5] As a matter of fact, if one reads the Latin translation of the *Sefer shorshe ha-qabbalah*, a lexicon of Kabbalistic terms, written in Arabic by the Spanish kabbalist Joseph Ibn Waqar in the fourteenth century, soon translated into Hebrew and, in 1486, into Latin by Flavius Mithridates for Giovanni Pico della Mirandola and now preserved at the Vatican Library,[6] one can verify that this bold statement

---

[4] "Per nomen Iod he uahu he, quod est nomen ineffabile quod dicunt Cabalistae futurum esse nomen messiae, evidenter cognoscitur futurum eum deum dei filium per spiritum sanctum hominem factum, et post eum ad perfectionem humani generis super homines paraclytum descensurum". Cf. Farmer, *Syncretism in the West*, 526-527.

[5] See M. Idel, "The Kabbalistic Backgrounds of the 'Son of God' in Giovanni Pico della Mirandola's Thought", in F. Lelli (ed.), *Giovanni Pico e la cabbalà* (Florence: Olschki, 2014) 19-45, on p. 37.

[6] Cf. Vat. ebr. 190, f. 253v. The reasoning is here indirect: the Messiah is identified with the *sefirah Tif'eret*, which in turn corresponds to the Tetragram. On f. 232v a peculiar translation could also have influenced Pico: the well-known passage from Proverbs 24:21 "Time dominum fili mi" (fear the Lord, my son), is rendered by Mithridates as "Time dominum filium meum", thus altering the perspective in a decisive way.

is partly confirmed in a possible interpretation, which is tendentious but in itself not impossible, of that text.

Yet, and here lies the surprise, if one were to judge the question as having been settled, the contents of the fourteenth thesis show that Pico meant something totally different. There, he clearly states that the Hebrew name of Jesus contains the letter *shin*, which is obviously lacking in the Tetragram. Let us read his words:

> By the letter <ש> that is, *shin*, which mediates in the name Jesus, it is indicated to us Cabalistically that the world then rested perfectly, as thoug in its perfection, when *Yod* was conjoined with *Vav* – which happened in Christ, who was the true Son of God, and man.[7]

Which is, then, the name of Jesus? The least one can say is that Pico assures us that he has a Kabbalistic explanation for the name and that it has two forms, which are mysteriously connected. One might suggest that, as Jesus is also called [the] Christ, by the same token Jesus has two Hebrew names which belong to him exclusively, or rather have been bestowed upon him by God alone: one is the Tetragram, belonging to him as Son of God and Messiah, and the other expressing his quality as the perfection of

---

[7] "Per litteram ש, id est scin, quae mediat in nomine Iesu, significatur nobis cabalistice quod tum perfecte quievit, tamquam in sua perfectione, mundus cum Iod coniunctus est cum Vau, quod factum est in Christo, qui fuit verus dei filius et homo". Cf. Farmer, *Syncretism in the West*, 526–527.

The Hebrew Names of Jesus in Renaissance Christian Kabbalah

creation. The exclusive character of these names, in other words the fact that no human being could be named after them, is a qualifying point, and it will resurface in later discussions on the biblical roots of Jesus' name. The other name, and the one which is only attributed to Jesus, is ישו (*Yeshu*), as one can deduce from the fourteenth conclusion that we have just quoted.

The intriguing characteristic of the latter name is that it is almost completely unknown in the Christian tradition. The medieval authors quoting in Latin transcription the name of Jesus (from Jerome to Isidore of Sevilla, from Bede the Venerable to Roger Bacon) refer to the form Iesua ישוע, that is to say a form that, as an abbreviation of Yehoshua', is documented several times in the Old Testament. This is also the form most frequently found, even in Hebrew characters, on the *tituli crucis* in Medieval iconography. The abbreviated form was confirmed, if we lend faith to the coeval transcriptions, since the Hebrew part of the inscription is now unreadable, after the discovery, announced in 1492 as a sensational event, of the 'authentic' relic of the *titulus crucis* itself, in the Roman Church of Santa Croce. The discovery, which was supposed to revive the effort for the liberation of the Holy Land and initiate a new crusade, immediately spread throughout Europe by means of the new media of the printing press.

One exception to the rule is the *titulus crucis* painted by Giotto, which can be admired at Santa Maria Novella in Florence. Very probably, this particular form of the name (ישו) can be explained by the fact that his graphic programme had been suggested by a Jew or a convert. The same unusual form is also found in the sacristy of Santo Spirito in Florence on a much later crucifix by Michelangelo.[8] As far as Pico is concerned, one might ask where this notion came from. If one does not want to imagine that he found it while contemplating Giotto's crucifix in Florence, which in turn was probably influenced by a Jewish informant, one has to suppose that he found it in the Jewish tradition, since it is the most widespread form of the name of Jesus used among the Jews.

If we assume that Pico trusted the Jewish tradition on this point, then we cannot but see at least two consequences: on the one hand, in this perspective Jewish tradition is not the object of suspicion or depreciation, it is rather utilised as a legitimate source for Christian theological considerations; on the other hand, considering that Pico inaugurated the tradition of Christian Kabbalah, it clearly emerges that its first motor was not philology but rather theology. Philology can rather be found at the end of the pioneering season of Jewish studies inaugurated by Christian Kabbalah.[9]

What was the source of the name Yeshu in the Jewish tradition? There are good reasons to surmise that this

---

[8] For the hypothesis that Michelangelo might have been influenced by Pico concerning the *titulus crucis* see G. Busi, *Michelangelo. Mito e solitudine del Rinascimento* (Milan: Mondadori, 2017), 43.

[9] See, for example, J. Drusius, *Decas Exercitationum theologicarum de vera pronunciatione nominis Jehova* (Utrecht, 1707). The last chapter is a philologically impeccable destruction of all we have recalled and we are going to say concerning a Hebrew name of Jesus different from ישוע.

particular form of the name has a polemical, anti-Christian origin. It presents, as a matter of fact, the advantage of omitting Jesus from the biblical tradition, in which the name Yeshu does not appear, and, at the same time, it makes it possible to encode in the very name a derogatory meaning, very probably a late interpretation but one of the utmost importance for Pico, who was interested precisely in the kind of alphabetical games he identified with the Kabbalah. The technique known as *notarikon*, that is the interpretation of a word as an acronym, makes it possible to hide an insult in the letters of the name: ימח שמו וזכרו, *Yimmach shemo u-zikro* (may his name and his memory be erased). This formula is not the worst found in the anti-Christian polemical tradition and it was certainly less vicious than the concurrent forms for Jesus such as *ha-taluy* (the hanged one), but more specific than the almost neutral *oto ha-ish* (that man).

It would be quite interesting to know whether Pico was aware of the polemical overtones attached to the name of his choice. Unfortunately, I am not able to answer this question with any certainty, but we know that his informant, Flavius Mithridates (Shemu'el ben Nissim Abulfaraǧ, alias Guglielmo Raimondo Moncada) shows in the glosses to his Hebrew-Latin translations a remarkable awareness of similar world-plays of polemical origin and to be particularly keen on this kind of coded or enigmatic polemics.[10]

---

[10] See S. Campanini, "Guglielmo Raimondo Moncada (alias Flavio Mitridate) traduttore di opere cabbalistiche", in M. Perani (ed.), *Guglielmo*

I have already published two examples of Mithridates' predilection for polemics, and it would not be difficult to find many more. One can refer to the ms. Vat. ebr. 189,[11] containing the Latin translation of the *Sha'ar ha-sod we-ha-emunah* (Gate of the Secret and of Faith), attributed to El'azar of Worms. Mithridates adds a gloss to the passage explaining the prayer '*Alenu le-shabbeach* (It is our duty to praise), specifically the polemical passage, often censored, in which one reads:

> It is our duty to praise the Master of all, to ascribe greatness to the Author of creation, who has not made us like the nations of the lands, nor placed us like the families of the earth, who has not made our portion like theirs, nor our destiny like all their multitudes. For they worship vanity and emptiness and pray to a God who cannot save.[12]

His remark refers to the gematria, the numerical correspondence between the expression וריק (emptiness), amounting to 316, and the number of the name of Jesus ישו. On the other hand, Mithridates does not comment on

---

Raimondo Moncada alias *Flavio Mitridate. Un ebreo converso siciliano* (Palermo: Officina di Studi Medievali, 2008) 49–88.

[11] On f. 525*v*.

[12] In Hebrew:
עלינו לשבח לאדון הכל, לתת גדלה ליוצר בראשית, שלא עשנו כגויי הארצות, ולא שמנו כמשפחות האדמה. שלא שם חלקנו כהם, וגרלנו ככל המונם, שהם משתחוים להבל וריק, ומתפללים לא אל אל יושיע.

the fact, perhaps because it is too obvious, that the expression לא יושיע (who does not save), contains very probably an anti-Christian allusion, hinting, at least implicitly, at the fact that the name of Jesus should be ישוע, etymologically tied to the root ישע (to save), only to deny then its contents. Moreover, in a gesture of ecumenical destructiveness, Mithridates adds that the following expression לאל לא (to a God that [...] not), whose numerical value is 92, corresponds perfectly to the name of the prophet of Islam, מחמד, Muhammad.[13]

In another passage (ms. Vat. ebr. 190), one finds an interesting observation in a gloss to the Kabbalistic commentary on Maimonides' *Guide of the Perplexed* by Abraham Abulafia, bearing the title *Sitre Torah*. Abulafia had written that the verse Deuteronomy 31:16 hid a prophetic allusion to Jesus: "This people will prostitute itself to the divinities of the foreign country". The numerical value of the expression "barbarous divinities" or "foreign gods", in Hebrew אלהי נכר, amounts once again to 316, just like ישו. Mithridates, in his gloss to this passage, comments that the secret contained in the biblical verse is greater than the Kabbalist thinks. If one also takes the following word הארץ (of the country), one obtains אלהי נכר הארץ, that is 612, corresponding to ישו ומרים (*Yeshu u-Miryam*), thus adding

---

[13] S. Campanini, "El'azar da Worms nelle traduzioni di Flavio Mitridate per Giovanni Pico della Mirandola", in M. Perani/G. Corazzol (ed.), *Flavio Mitridate mediatore fra culture nel contesto dell'ebraismo siciliano del XV secolo* (Palermo: Officina di Studi Medievali, 2012) 47–80, on pp. 60-61.

the Virgin to this coded prophecy. A couple of years later, surprisingly, this very gematria will be published by a baptised Jew of Spanish origin, Pablo de Heredia, in his *Epistula de secretis*, without any allusion to Abulafia, as proof that the passage should not be understood polemically but as a positive prophecy of the triumph of Christianity, adding that 612 also corresponds to the word ברית, *berit*, the Covenant.[14] One can beg the question as to whether Pico, identifying in Yeshu the Hebrew name of Jesus, was not following a similar logic. It would even be possible to attribute the idea of reversing the polemical value inscribed in this form of the name to Mithridates himself, since his conversion had been opportunistic, as he confesses in his glosses, and his personal attitude had been inspired by a remarkably modern indifference in matters of religion, a position which was certainly extraneous to Pico, but which would explain how his teacher could manage to use polemical and propagandistic tools for and against Christianity without the shadow of any moral inhibition. A pious model for this providential reversion of the polemical sting could be found in the biblical figure of Balaam, who wanted to curse and was forced, against his will, to bless.

Be that as it may, Pico was firmly convinced that the true name of Jesus was Yeshu ישו, and that this name did

---

[14] S. Campanini, "Talmud, Philosophy, Kabbalah: A Passage from Pico della Mirandola's Apologia and its Source", in M. Perani (ed.), *The Words of a Wise Man's Mouth are Gracious. Festschrift for Günter Stemberger on the Occasion of His 65th Birthday* (Berlin/New York: De Gruyter, 2005) 429–447.

not hide any curse, as the Jews believed, but precisely the mystery of his human and divine nature if we assume, as it is very likely, that he was well aware of it.

Nevertheless, a problem is left unresolved concerning the relationship, stated but not explained by Pico, between Jesus' name and the Tetragram. On this point, Johannes Reuchlin, a follower of Pico, reopens the discussion in his dialogue *De verbo mirifico*, published in Basle in 1494, the year of Pico's death. Reuchlin suggests combining the two names in order to obtain a third, synthetic one. This construction of an unheard name, obscurely anticipated by Nicolaus of Cues in a sermon (*Dies sanctificatus*) and by Paul of Burgos in his supplements to the *Postilla* of Nicolaus of Lyra,[15] represents Reuchlin's most significant contribution to the formation of a Christian Kabbalah. His proposition, however, would not be universally accepted, as we shall see. This holds true even if, as Robert Wilkinson has shown,[16] there had been much earlier attempts in the same direction, I am thinking in particular about a remote fragment of a certain Evagrius (identified hypothetically with the theologian Evagrius Ponticus), already suggesting in late antiquity that the

---

[15] Cf. B.P. Copenhaver, "Lefèvre d'Étaples, Symphorien Champier and the Secret Names of God", *Journal of the Warburg and Courtauld Institutes* 40 (1977) 189-211.

[16] R.J. Wilkinson, *Tetragrammaton: Western Christians and the Hebrew Name of God. From the Beginnings to the Seventeenth Century* (Leiden/Boston: Brill, 2014) see also my review of this book in *Materia Giudaica* 20-21 (2015-2016) 497-500.

letter *shin* was bound to make the ineffable Tetragram pronounceable.

Reuchlin, who had visited Florence during a diplomatic mission in 1490, in order to see Pico and to ask him for some clarifications concerning his Kabbalistic allusions, wanted to eliminate the apparently contradictory statements of the *Theses*, developing a peculiar form of the name of Jesus, which was certainly unheard-of but destined to enjoy a long life. One can remark, incidentally, that the formation of this name serves as very convincing proof of what was suggested above: at the beginning of Christian Kabbalah, which was in turn the matrix of Jewish studies among the Christians, there is not philology, but a kind of mysticism of names, and a highly creative one at that. Grammar needed to be respected, but at best as a means to an aim that goes far beyond pure philology. Precisely on this point, paradoxically, Reuchlin reveals that he is an authentic Kabbalist: in order to justify his innovations, he displays a re-discovery of Scripture and of the *depositum fidei*. What seems to be the *non plus ultra* of conservatism, or moderate reformism, veils an innovative potential and a creative energy of a rarely equalled radicality.

Apparently, Reuchlin does little more than put the letter *shin* in the middle of the Tetragram and create the unprecedented name IHSUH ((יהשוה, destined to become remarkably widespread. This mysterious name will not be as popular as the monogram IHS promoted in the fifteenth century by Bernardino da Feltre, but it will resurface time and again in later literature, even becoming a commercial logo in the typographical mark of the publishing house of Thomas Anshelm, in Pforzheim, Stuttgart, Hagenau and Tubingen.[17]

Reuchlin, on the other hand, was not only a very prominent Christian Kabbalist but also, at the same time, the founder of modern Jewish studies and of Hebrew bibliography.[18] For this reason, together with Pico, he was obliged to explain how the name of Jesus was also connected to the idea of salvation and to the biblical name of Joshua. He was very well aware of the fact that in the Bible at least five different figures bear the name Jesus/Joshua, among others Jesus ben Sira. The name Joshua, he writes, had been imposed on the patriarch by Moses and not by God. For him, Joshua is a mere *figura Christi* and, considering that his name alludes to salvation, it is, according to Maimonides' morphology of divine names, a function name and not an essential name. The true essential name (IHSUH), however, is not found explicitly in the Bible and can only be detected behind coded allusions. The virtue of this name, according to Reuchlin, is to make the ineffable Tetragram pronounceable. Moreover, and consequently,

---

[17] H. Alberts, "Reuchlins Drucker, Thomas Anshelm. Mit besonderer Berücksichtigung seiner Pforzheimer Presse", in M. Krebs (ed.), *Johannes Reuchlin. Festgabe 1955* (Sigmaringen: Thorbecke, 1994) 205–265.

[18] Cf. S. Campanini, "Wege in die Stadt der Bücher. Ein Beitrag zur Geschichte der hebräischen Bibliographie (die katholische bibliographische „Dynastie" Iona-Bartolocci-Imbonati)", in P. Schäfer/I. Wandrey (ed.), *Reuchlin und seine Erben. Forscher, Denker, Ideologen und Spinner* (Ostfildern: Thorbecke, 2005) 61–76.

this is the only name of Jesus that truly performs miracles (*verbum mirificum*).

The numerical value of the IHSUH name is 326, that is 10 more than the name Yeshu. To make things even more complicated, Reuchlin writes that the name corresponds, according to some "Kabbalistic calculations", to the Hebrew words meaning 'image', 'cross', 'wood' (*lignum*), 'your countenance', which, invariably, correspond to 160 (צלם, צלם, עץ, פניך). How are we supposed to arrive at the figure 326? If one takes these words in pairs, connected by the conjunction we- (ו) 'and', one obtains exactly 326 (for example עץ ופניך, 'wood and your countenance' gives 326, which is the numerical value of יהשוה). In avoiding explaining himself too clearly, Reuchlin suggests a mysterious relationship between the Pentagram (IHSUH) and the cross. Some Christian Kabbalists of the second generation will try to explain this relationship, as we will see.

At the same time, Reuchlin proposes a scheme of the history of salvation which is supposed to account for the 'change of name' of God, according to the synthetic formula: "in natura SDI (Shadday, 3 letters), in lege ADNI (Adonay, 4 letters) in charitate IHSUH (5 letters)". This divine pedagogy, modelled on the Talmudic "prophecy of Elijah" (*oraculum Eliae*), articulating the entire course of history in three epochs: nature, law and the Messiah, made it possible to retrieve, at the end of the fifteenth century, a novel messianic terminology while referring, at the same time, to its prestigious antiquity. The very idea of revelation implies, as a matter of fact, a reception, meaning that the new could be as worthy as, or even better than, the ancient. From this vantage point, the Renaissance mentality was decidedly more complex than it is sometimes depicted, that is to say, as if its main preoccupation were antiquity, access to the original sources or the restoration of the ancient church. Even a decisive event in modern history such as the Reformation is not entirely comprehensible if it is removed from its Renaissance context, thereby failing to appreciate the innovative energy of an intellectual movement such as the Christian Kabbalah, which only apparently aimed to restore the authentic message of revelation.

Although Reuchlin's knowledge of Kabbalistic literature at the time of the publication of his second book on the topic, the *De arte cabalistica* (1517),[19] increased significantly, as the Kabbalistic bibliography appended to the volume demonstrates, what remained unchanged was the fact that Jesus' name was still at the core of his presentation of Kabbalah as an exegetical technique (*ars*). Reuchlin's correspondence[20] reveals that many of the readers of the *De verbo mirifico* complained about his obscurity concerning the name and repeatedly asked him to offer some further explanations. In comparison to the much earlier *De verbo mirifico*, Reuchlin did try to explain himself more clearly in the *De arte cabbalistica*, multiplying his attempts to find prophetic evocations of his peculiar form of Jesus' names

---

[19] J. Reuchlin, *L'arte cabbalistica. De arte cabalistica*, ed. by G. Busi/S. Campanini (Florence: Opus Libri, 1996).
[20] J. Reuchlin, *Briefwechsel*, ed. by S. Rhein/M. Dall'Asta/G. Dörner (4 vol.; Stuttgart/Bad Cannstatt: Frommann/Holzboog, 1999–2013).

at selected biblical passages, even if one cannot escape the impression that they are rather *a posteriori* constructions. The secret revelation of the miraculous name IHSUH is inserted in a peculiar narrative involving the angel Raziel, sent by God to console Adam after the fall. The promise of redemption is thus embedded in an historical perspective justifying the progressive revelation of the name.

As we have recalled, neither Pico's form of the name of Jesus, nor its variant proposed by Reuchlin, were universally accepted. One example may illustrate this fact: in the *Libellus Hora faciendi pro Domino*, a Hebrew primer published in Tubingen in 1513 by the baptised Jew of Spanish origin, Matthaeus Adriani, who called himself a "magnus cabalista", the author attacked a Hebrew translation of the *Ave Maria*, published on a broadsheet that appeared in print in 1508 by yet another baptised Jew, the German Johannes Pfefferkorn,[21] the arch-enemy of Johannes Reuchlin during the battle of the Hebrew books from 1509 onwards. Adriani criticised, among other things, the form chosen by Pfefferkorn of the Hebrew name of Jesus. Pfefferkorn translated into Hebrew (very probably from Latin) the name of Jesus using the form usually found in the *titulus crucis*, ישוע, but Adriani counters:

> For Jesus Christ I have used the form "Iesus massia" (משיח ישוש), because the other translation, Joshua, is not correct

---

[21] Cf. J. Adams/C. Heß (ed.), *Revealing the Secrets of the Jews. Johannes Pfefferkorn and Christian Writings About Jewish Life and Literature in Early Modern Europe* (Berlin/Boston: De Gruyter, 2018).

and changes things unduly. Joshua is the name of a man, who was called Hosea, servant of Moses [...] We have written Yesus since that is his name in the books of the Talmud and in the Book of victory (*Sefer ha-Nitztzachon*) and in the book of the generations of Jesus the Nazarene (*Sefer Toledot Yeshu ha-notzri*) and, if God permits it, we will write on this topic in Latin.[22]

Adriani never wrote (or published) the promised book, but it is quite clear that, at the time, he wanted to please his protector Reuchlin by attacking his enemy and confuting his ideas about the name of Jesus. On the other hand, he does not quote the name consisting in five letters, but the polemical name also found in Pico della Mirandola, which was not, as we shall see, completely foreign to Reuchlin, either. The peculiar Hebrew form of the name of Jesus he suggested was a kind of compromise, according to the endings (against the rules of the Hebrew language) to Latin syntax. Therefore, he uses not only the already strange יְשׁוּשׁ, but also a stunning accusative Yesum (יְשׁוּם). This surprising choice did

---

[22] "Et pro Iesus christus posui Iesus massia. In alia translatione legitur Iosue pro Iesu quae videtur esse magna mutatio, quia Iosue est nomen viri qui prius vocabatur hosea Moysi minister... nos posuimus Iesu, quia semper ita vocatum invenimus in thalmudicis libris et in libro victoriae qui vocatur Cefer nitzachon et in libro nativitatis Iesu hanozri quod significat Iesus nazarenus, de quo nomine deo dante aliquid latinum faciemus brevi tempore". M. Adriani, *Libellus hora faciendi pro domino* (Tübingen: Anshelm, 1513), ff. DIIv–DIIIr.

not earn Adriani much consideration, although he was able to have a remarkable, albeit short, career as the first professor of Hebrew at the Collegium Trilingue in Leuven (1517-1519), and later in Wittenberg (1520-1521). Very soon, he seems to have developed some doubts about the correct form of Jesus' name, as appears from two letters, one in Hebrew and one in Latin, which he sent to the Augustinian friar Caspar Amman.[23]

One of the Christian Kabbalists who criticised Adriani vehemently, without naming him explicitly, was the most important after Pico and Reuchlin, that is to say the observant Franciscan Franciscus Georgius (Francesco Zorzi) of Venice. In his *De harmonia mundi* (1525) he fiercely defends the name ישו as the only correct one, and an entire chapter of his large work (II, 6,8) is dedicated to criticising the alternatives that had been suggested. The right Hebrew name of Jesus is, in his view, without doubt ישו and, in order to prove this, he recurs to a double Kabbalistic strategy. On the one hand, he quotes, as a prophecy, a verse from the Psalms (96:11-12):

ישמחו השמים ותגל הארץ ירעם הים ומלאו יעלוז שדי וכל [אשר בו]
(May the heavens rejoice and the earth be joyful, the sea and what it contains! May the fields burst with happiness with what is on them).

---

[23] See S. Campanini, "Una lettera in ebraico e una in latino da Matthaeus Adriani a Caspar Amman sul nome di Gesù", *Bruniana & Campanelliana* 24, 1 (2018) 25-47.

The Hebrew Names of Jesus in Renaissance Christian Kabbalah

If one takes the initials of these words, the result is יהוה יהו ישו, that is to say the plastic representation of the transformation of the Tetragram into the name of Jesus. On this basis, he criticises the opinion of some (*aliqui*), that is to say Reuchlin and his followers, who thought the name of Jesus was to be found by inserting the letter *shin* into the heart of the Tetragram. Zorzi opines that the two letters *he* (ה) of the Tetragram are conflated into one (in accordance with the esoteric doctrine of the Kabbalistic *Sefer ha-Temunah*, containing such letter manipulations) and reversed to form a *shin* (ש).[24] In order to prove his contention, Zorzi

---

[24] "Et nomen redemptoris nostri scribi deberet tribus literis tantummodo ipsius plenis mysteriis scilicet ישי. Nec addenda est litera ה combinata, ut aliqui opinati sunt, quia illae iam (ut diximus) conversae sunt in ש. Nec apponendum est secundum ש dicendo שושי quamvis Latine dicatur, sic exquirente ordine declinationis grammaticalis, de quo non multum curan | dum est, quia mysteria non sunt in idiomate Latino, sed Hebraeo, ubi attendendum est, ne aliquid addatur, vel minuatur, quia multa destruerentur mysteria, quae tam in significatis literarum illius nominis, quam in numeris earum, et etiam in vaticiniis correspondentibus continentur, ex quibus aliqua vel pauca percurremus. Habent pro constanti secretiores theologi, quod oracula multoties continent nomina illorum, de quibus prophetatur, in principio, fine, vel medio dictionum, secundum quem modum nomen Messiaeh saepius reperitur, ut in versiculo psalmi septuagesimi primi: Ante solem permanet nomen eius, et beneficentur in ipso omnes tribus terrae. Nomen enim ושי Iesu continetur in capitibus horum verborum, permanet nomen eius, et benedicentur, quae in Hebraeo sic dicunt: וכרבתיו ומש וני inin semo veitbarcu, ubi si accipiantur capita dictionum, quae sunt ו ש י constituunt ושי Iesu, quod nomen fuit ante solem, et in ipso benedictae sunt omnes gentes. Similiter in libro Geneseos capite 49 / ubi dicitur: Veniat Messiah, et ipsi congregabuntur, capita dictionum constituunt nomen Iesu, quae in Hebraeo sic dicunt

quotes two more verses: in Psalms 71:17, one reads: "May his name live forever, his fame grow under the sun, may one wish to be as blessed as he is, may all peoples proclaim his bliss". The words ינון שמו ויברכו, give once more, if one takes only the initials, the name ישו, and he combines this with the messianic prophecy of Genesis 49: "Shilo will come [and the peoples will gather around him]": יבא שילה ולו, once again bringing the same result, the initials of this sentence are read as ישו. According to Zorzi, the name Yeshush, preferred, as we have seen, by Adriani, is simply wrong, since the second *shin* is only a Latin morphological ending. The mysteries (or sacraments, as he calls them), however, are never in Latin, but only in Hebrew, which he considers the original language of creation and the ur-language of humankind. Zorzi follows up his argument by stating that the name Yeshu is perfect, since it contains the unities (6), the tens (10) and the hundreds (300) and, if one discards the zeros, one has the 10 (3+1+6), a perfect number, corresponding to the *sefirot*, a clear demonstration, in his view, of the identity between Jesus and God. The *yod* (the first letter of the name), whose numerical value is ten, is God, the *waw* (6) is the Spirit, since in Hebrew the letter *waw* is the conjunction (and, or *et*), the link between the Father and the Son, whereas the letter *shin*, the initial of the word Shabbat is, in accordance with Pico's

---

אבי הליש ולו iabo silo velo. Capita enim sunt י ש et ו, quae literae collocatae ordine Hebraico reddunt ושי". F. Zorzi, *L'armonia del mondo*, ed. by S. Campanini (Milan: Bompiani 2010), 1614-1616.

Theses, the peace, the end of creation and its completion. One can even harmonise this name with the etymologies of the Hebrew letters according to Jerome's *Liber nominum Hebraicorum*: *yod* is in fact the beginning (*principium*), *waw* means *he himself* (in Hebrew *hu'*), and *shin* is intended as the perfection (*perfectio*). According to this reading, the meaning of the name could be contained in the sentence from the Apocalypse: "I am the A and the O".[25]

For Zorzi, as for his disciples of the Franciscan Observance, heterogeneous explanations are not contradictory, provided that they converge towards one unifying goal. It is for this reason that the letter *waw* can also be interpreted as *arbor vitae* or Tree of Life, the life in which, according to the poet Aratus, quoted by Paul in the *Acts of the Apostles*, "we live, we move ourselves and we are".[26]

---

[25] Rev 22:13.

[26] "Sed mirabilius est in psalmo nonagesimo quinto in verbis illis: Laetentur coeli, et exultet terra, contremiscat mare, et omnis plenitudo eius, exultabunt campi, et omnia, quae in eis sunt. In quorum verborum capitibus habetur nomen quadriliterum completum, et postea idem nomen absque ultimo ה, deinde nomen Iesu ad denotandum, quod quadriliterum illud complecti debebat in nomine Iesu, tamquam successore suo, cui quodammodo cedebat, quia virtus illius nominis quadriliteri data est Iesu, cui Pater omnia dedit. Unde probat author Sepher temunot per illud ה ultimum ipsius nominis quadriliteri, divinitatem debere uniri cum humanitate, et effici Messiah, in quo existeret virtus illius magni nominis. Ideo uniuntur nomina, et succedit nomen Iesu, incompleto illo quadrilitero, quando secundo repetitur, quia sicut in priori testimonio venerabantur completum, sic in secundo, et ultimo cessisse innuitur (ut diximus) nostro Iesu. Verba enim Hebraea textus illius psalmi sic habentur הַיָּם וּמְלֹאוֹ יַעֲלֹז שָׂדַי וְכָל יִשְׂמְחוּ הַשָּׁמַיִם וְתָגֵל הָאָרֶץ יִרְעַם. Quarum dictionum

Saverio Campanini

The same explanation of Pico della Mirandola's intentions is found in a hitherto unpublished commentary to Pico's *Theses*, based on Zorzi's lectures in 1539, copied in 1555 and preserved in Jerusalem.[27] One finds there a discussion concerning the difference between the name Yeshua', a merely human name, and Yeshu, a unique name, belonging to Christ only. This proves that it is a divine name, not deriving, like Saviour, Lord or Almighty, from his attributes, according to Maimonides' line of thought,

capita ordine Hebraeo posita sunt ישו יהו יהוה. Sed postquam de literis nominis Iesu pertractamus, opportunum existimavi explicare etiam quod ex literarum interpretatione plures literae in illo reperiri non debeant, cum istae perfecte important ea, quae continentur in nominato per hoc nomen יֵשׁוּ. Nam י principium significat ו ipse, שׁ principium sabat innuens ipsum requiem, et finem. Denotant igitur, quod ipse est principium, finis, et requies omnium, sicut in Apocalypsi ipsemet ait: Ego sum α et ω, principium et finis. Et cum in his verbis omnia includantur, sufficiunt illae literae, neque aliae debent apponi. Completur insuper hoc nomen יֵשׁוּ ex numero maiori, minori, et medio in denarium, qui est numerus completus. Est enim senarius, unus denarius, et tres centenarii, qui simul iuncti constituunt decem, numerum quidem perfectum, et constitutum ex omnibus generibus rerum, spiritualium videlicet, coelestium, et terrestrium, quae importantur per numeros, denarios, | et centenarios, iuxta illud, quod Paulus saepius repetit dicens: In ipso est omnis plenitudo, et in ipso reconciliantur omnia". Zorzi, *L'armonia del mondo*, 1616-1619.

[27] Ms. Yahudah, Var. 24. On this manuscript see C. Wirszubski, "Francesco Giorgio's Commentary on Giovanni Pico's Kabbalistic Theses", *Journal of the Warburg and Courtauld Institutes* 37 (1974) 145-156; F. Secret, "Notes pour l'histoire des juifs en France et les hébraïsants chrétiens", *Revue des Etudes Juives* 134 (1975) 81-100; on this and some other manuscript containing the same work, see S. Campanini, "Il commento alle *Conclusiones cabalisticae* nel Cinquecento", in Lelli (ed.), *Giovanni Pico e la cabbalà*, 167-230.

The Hebrew Names of Jesus in Renaissance Christian Kabbalah

but, exactly like the Tetragram, an essential name, a proper name in a sense which goes far beyond the grammatical meaning of the term.[28]

The next generation of Christian Kabbalists was faced with a deeply changed cultural and theological climate, due to the Reformation and Counter-Reformation and to the renewed persecutions of the Jews and their books, which took place from 1553 onwards. Nevertheless, many of them did try to pursue the reflection on the name of Jesus, increasing its syncretic potential both in depth and extension. A case in point is undoubtedly that of the Franciscan Observant Arcangelo da Borgonovo, the first to publish a book on Christian Kabbalah in Italian, dedicated entirely to the name of Jesus, bearing the title *Specchio di salute. Dechiaratione sopra il nome di Giesù secondo gli Hebrei cabalisti, Greci, Caldei, Persi et Latini* (Mirror of Salvation. Explanation of the name of Jesus according to the Kabbalist Jews, the Greeks, the Chaldeans, the Persians and the Latins), which appeared in print in Ferrara in 1557. Arcangelo, who had been a pupil of Francesco Zorzi, tries to show, or rather to express openly, what his teacher had only hinted at, namely that the names יהשוה and ישו are not

---

[28] "Nota tamen quod multi in scriptura sacra vocati fuere ישוע Iesuah, sed nusquam invenitur, quod quis vocatus fuerit Iesum, nec ante, nec post Christum, quia est nomen divinitatis. Nullus autem habuit divinitatem preter ipsum Christum. Iesus ergo dictus fuit hoc nomine a divinitate, non autem ab ethimologia vocabuli, secundum quam idem est quod Salvator, quia idem esset Iesuah, quod Iesus, ישוע Iesuah enim dicitur a verbo ישע, quod salvavit significat". Ms. Yahudah, Var. 24, f. 55r.

contradictory or alternative: the letter *shin*, if reversed, still contains the two *he* of the Tetragram.[29] As one can see, the conciliation not only intends to diminish the divergences between Reuchlin and Zorzi, but also aims consistently to make sense of Pico's enigmatic contentions.

A final question, which is inescapable for any reader of the *De verbo mirifico*, no less than of the *De arte cabalistica*, must be raised in lieu of a conclusion: why does Reuchlin speak repeatedly of a secret and recur to the language of secrecy if the name IHSUH is mentioned explicitly more than once? Moreover, how did he see the compatibility between his peculiar form of the name and the one found in his authoritative source, that is to say Pico della Mirandola? Another convert of Spanish origin, but born in Provence, Todros ha-Kohen, called Lodovico Carretto after his baptism, in his apologetic letter bearing the title *Liber visorum divinorum*, published in Paris in Hebrew and Latin in 1553, relates that he converted to Christianity after a miraculous vision, already evoked in the title of his pamphlet. Carretto declares that he saw the key, a metaphor also to be taken literally, allowing him to reconcile the name ישו proposed by Pico and the name יהשוה, suggested by Reuchlin.

---

[29] A. da Borgonovo, *Dechiaratione sopra il nome di Giesù, secondo gli Hebrei cabalisti, Greci, Caldei, Persi, & Latini* יהוה ישו *Intitolato Specchio di Salute, alla molto illustre Signora Taddea Malaspina Dedicata* (Ferrara: Francesco Rossi, 1557), 211v–212r.

The Hebrew Names of Jesus in Renaissance Christian Kabbalah

The simple graphic disposition seems to offer, in an elementary way, which might also seem very artificial, depending on the taste of the reader, the solution to the problem we have tried to tackle. If one reads the letters around the centre, one has the Tetragram, the vertical line gives the name ישו, the horizontal line has השה, meaning the Lamb, all the letters taken together form the Reuchlinian pentagram, and the very form of this crossword puzzle, designs precisely a cross, presenting not only a pleasing calligram but a compelling solution to the riddles Reuchlin had left unanswered concerning the name of Jesus and the mystery of the cross. Carretto declared that this vision led him to his conversion and, even if his words do not seem very convincing to the modern reader, his contemporaries, while skeptic, had to accept the fact that at least one Jew had been converted by these crossword puzzles. It was not to be excluded that some others of his brethren might be affected by the very same eccentric logic. As we have recalled, the *Liber visorum divinorum* was not only written in Hebrew, but also had a Latin version on the front page. Thus, its author did not abandon the hope, shared by all the Christian Kabbalists of the Renaissance, to convert not only Jews to Christianity but also Christians to Kabbalah.[30]

The Hebrew name of Jesus has, as we have been able to show, a history, and the resistance to these mystical or Kabbalistic speculations on the name of Jesus and their critique also has a prestigious historical lineage. In his *Praise of Folly* (not in the first edition of 1511 but starting from the Strasburg edition of 1514)[31] Erasmus already relates, addressing his friend Thomas More, that he once heard in England an octogenarian theologian from Scotland preaching that the letter shin in the Tetragram has a very profound theological meaning. In actual fact, Erasmus comments, since he was Scottish, he pronounced the word sin as if it were shin and this was assumed to be the proof that Jesus came to save us from our sins.[32] Erasmus'

---

[30] See S. Campanini, "Nottole ad Atene. La qabbalah cristiana e la conversione degli ebrei", *Materia Giudaica* 29 (2014) 81–101.

[31] Cf. C.H. Miller (ed.), *Moriae Encomium id est Stultitiae Laus* (Ord. IV, t. III of *Opera Omnia Desiderii Erasmi Roterodami*; Amsterdam/Oxford: North-Holland Publishing Company, 1979), 164.

[32] "Auditus est a nobis alius quidam octogenarius, adeo Theologus, ut in hoc Scotum ipsum renatum putes. Is explicaturus mysterium nominis Iesu, mira subtilitate demonstravit in ipsis litteris latere, quidquid de illo dici possit. Etenim quod tribus dumtaxat inflectitur casibus, id manifestum esse simulacrum divini ternionis. Deinde quod prima vox Iesus, desinat in s. secunda Iesum in m, tertia Iesu in u, in hoc arrêton subesse mysterium: nempe tribus litterulis indicantibus eum esse summum, medium, et ultimum. Restabat mysterium his quoque retrusius, Mathematica ratione. Iesus sic in duas aequales diffidit portiones, ut scilicet pentemimeres in medio resideret. Deinde docuit eam litteram apud Hebraeos esse quam illi Syn appellent: porro syn Scotorum, opinor,

devastating irony may be amusing but it does not hide that the questions raised by the present excursus are thus left unanswered. If the idea of the holiness of Scripture has to be taken seriously, the dispute between those who attribute it solely to the contents of Revelation and those who cannot separate it from its material, linguistic or esthetic form is not destined to be settled in the near future. It would, indeed, be very easy to identify this debate with the secular struggle between church and synagogue, since the rift runs throughout Christianity itself and even the Christian Kabbalists could not reach an agreement on the form of the Hebrew name of Jesus among themselves, although they shared the general view of the importance of the Kabbalah as a confirmation of the main tenets of the Christian faith. The eccentric perspective gained from the present vantage point might contribute to appreciating an almost forgotten, yet living, heritage of Renaissance creativity in religious issues.

---

lingua, peccatum sonat: atque hinc palam declarari, Iesum esse qui peccata tolleret mundi". Erasmi Roterodami, *Μωρίας ἐγκώμιον, id est Stultitiae laus, Libellus vere aureus, nec minus eruditus, et salutaris, quam festivus, nuper ex ipsius autoris archetypis diligentissime restitutus* (Argentorati: Ex aedibus Schurerianis, 1514), gIIv.

A Productive Coexistence for Theology and Religious Studies. What Kind of Work is Needed on Both Sides?
Pierre Gisel

1. *A Proposal*

My title expresses an objective: a possible,[1] even desirable and productive, coexistence for both sides present.

My title also recognises the dual existence, of theology on one side and religious studies on the other. It does not announce a fusion of disciplines, or a homogenisation of the place of enquiry nor a transformation of theology into religious studies (or a subordination of religious studies to a theology, the current model of the latter therefore being modified).

---

[1] The present submission reiterates, with some modifications, and at the invitation of Alberto Melloni, a presentation given at Trento on 3 July 2015 (the fortieth anniversary of the founding of the Centro per le Scienze Religiose, Fondazione Bruno Kessler), which was published in the *Annali di studi religiosi* 17 (2016) 53-65. I would like to thank my colleague Christophe Chalamet of the University of Geneva for his careful review of this English translation and his suggestions for improvement. Portuguese translation: "Uma coexistência criativa entre a teologia e as ciências das religiões: que trabalho desenvolver dos dois lados?", in F.V. Campos/F. Senra/T.A. de Almeida (ed.), *A epistemologia das Ciências da Religião: pressupostos, questões e desafios* (Curitiba, Brazil: CRV, 2018).

Pierre Gisel

2. A Contentious Background

It is well-known that the relationship between theology, on the one hand, and religious studies on the other, is more often than not contentious. Fraught with issues of secularity, secularisation, the "escape from religion" (Marcel Gauchet) and conflicts between church and state – emblematic in France – to which are added, or mingled, the criticism of religion, whether it be scientific (during the Enlightenment), or political (from the *Priestertrugtheorie* to Karl Marx onward), psychological (from Sigmund Freud to cognitive psychology), or cultural (Friedrich Nietzsche and many others). In concrete terms, the academic institutions and organisations studying and researching the religious field are marked by these.[2]

In terms of recurrent conflicts, variously present according to time or place, it seems to me that several types of debate can be distinguished.

---

[2] The faculty which I frequented went from being a Faculty of Protestant Theology, according to the traditional university model from the nineteenth century, to becoming a Faculty of Religious Studies, but the process remained incomplete, the Faculty being unable to truly develop in social relevance and experiencing some reversions, which revealed the fact that some issues and options were not sufficiently clarified. It was the seat of a dispute, which is a case in point and which, beyond the conflicts between the institutions or the various players involved, was riddled with a great many fundamentally instructive questions; cf. on this subject my booklet, *Traiter du religieux à l'Université. Une dispute socialement révélatrice* (Lausanne: Éditions Antipodes, 2011).

a) Neutrality or Commitment

An initial conflict can be seen between scientific neutrality, which is assumed to be that of religious studies, and the committed, confessional nature of theology, the latter being, moreover, in academic units linked to the Church, subsequently feeding the suspicion – or, as the case may be, the specific validation – that theologians must therefore be "organic intellectuals" (Antonio Gramsci), placing the interests of their institution or their militancy ahead of a respect for truth and honesty in the debate.

In the light of this background, many now seek to question what would naïvely pass for scientific objectivity, by calling upon a sociology or a history of science, to relativistic ends. Personally, it seems to me that the conclusions thus drawn are often too radical and insufficiently differentiated: the issue of what should, or could, be understood according to scientific objectivity must certainly be reworked and dealt with in depth, but we must do so without any disqualification put forward on the simple pretext that no one is neutral or that evidence varies according to the history or indeed the areas of civilisation.

Meanwhile, many now seek to reassert the value of the right to conviction and give it a place, but here again, if the point must indeed be reiterated and reworked, it must be done, in my opinion, according to several clarifications of the defined frameworks and relevancies and once more, without any radicalising conclusions.

A note regarding the psychology of mindsets may be added here: in the modern era, particularly in the latter half of the nineteenth century, religious studies were often born within Protestant faculties of theology (German, Dutch and Swiss) and underwent, or are still undergoing, development as a process of progressive emancipation, as yet unfinished in their eyes. This explains the suspicious watchfulness and recurring statements claiming that they are fundamentally different from theology, their very make-up emphasising the need to differentiate between them.

b) Religious Plurality or the Pursuit of a Defined Tradition
A second conflict can be observed concerning the presence and growing awareness of religious plurality, which religious studies inherently honour, whereas theology would seek to cover the whole field with the intention of considering it an ultimate authority, or indeed regulating it against the backdrop of a unique tradition, even if that single tradition is internally diverse and has experienced historical changes or interruptions.

However, let it be said here that the advent of religious studies carries far more than an awareness of religious plurality. Consequently, the opposition between religious studies and theology (or overcoming it for the purpose of peaceful coexistence) cannot be resolved by setting up multi-confessional academic platforms – faculties, departments and others – or by integrating multi-confessionalism or the diversity of traditions (Judaism, Islam, Hinduism, Buddhism, Taoism, Confucianism and many more besides Christianity) into their work, even if dialogue, discussion, indeed interaction, can fruitfully take place with such a background.

c) A Shift or Decentering of the Facts and Questions
With regard to the field in which theology is developing, it is important to recognise – and this opens up a third type of debate – that religious studies are bringing about a shift or a decentring. This is not only because their types of questions are different rather than homologous. It is also because religious things are no longer, in their view, a subject or a field which will always remain the same, observable in a definable territory, whatever the historical times or areas of civilisation, the only difference being the ways of filling in or acting in the boxes drawn within this territory (the box for God or a reference to an ultimate authority; the meditation, symbolisation, rituality, community or church boxes, the foundation or origins box, the regulation box, etcetera).

To begin with, it is important to bear in mind that not all forms of religion develop a theology, and this phenomenon is not circumstantial but related to different types of religion. Furthermore, it is important to remember that what is understood by religion is open to debate, particularly with regard to the question of whether religion leads to proper community or ecclesiastical organisation or not. Let us keep to what is said by both major references on the subject in our history, *relegere* on the one hand (the human virtue of stepping back from the enormity of the cosmos and gathering the signs within it to be interpreted – the opposite virtue to *hubris*) which Cicero summarised at the end of pre-Christian Antiquity, and *religare* on the other hand (a vertical connection to transcendence and a horizontal connection, constituting community or sociality).

The latter has indeed been progressively favoured by Christianity and the West,[3] to be ultimately the only interpretation evoked in modern times,[4] with the exception of esoterisms. There is also the question of what, if any, distinction should be made between religion as culture (in ancient India, cultural patrimony and religious heritage were indissociable, as were the symbolic and the religious in so-called primitive societies studied by anthropologists),[5] and religion as politics (the theologico-political has a limited history, both in terms of its emergence and its fate).

3. *Theologising Once Again Correlated to Particularity and Subjected to Critical Trial*

Among the various religious studies, anthropology, born out of the meeting of different cultural systems (following

---

[3] However, Thomas Aquinas, for example, in his *Summa Theologica* (1266–1273), IIa IIae, q. 81–100, developed a short treatise on religion which echoes in every way Cicero's views (the *religare* was, on the other hand, honoured by Lactantius or Saint Augustine for example).

[4] Emile Durkheim recognises this in *The Elementary Forms of the Religious Life* (London: George Allen & Unwin Ltd., 1912) both when he defines religion as a 'belief system' and when he asserts that there is no religion without 'Church', which is both typical and false.

[5] Note that here, the religious field is not bound by a distinction between what is canonical or non-canonical and that this distinction probably goes hand in hand with a religious field that is separate and, as such, tied to heterogeneity or transcendence.

the modern discoveries of Asia, Latin America, Oceania and Africa), has highlighted the extent to which non-Christian and non-monotheistic cultures lived primarily according to processes of negotiation with the world and beyond (strangeness, death, borders, otherness, etcetera), negotiations which were repeated through ritual practice.[6] This is a different perspective from that of an order of meaning, supported and nourished by religion.

Very differently, theology, whatever its kind, appears here linked to the setting up of an order of meaning, with its organisation into a system, invested with human intelligibility (the question of God, of his death or substitutes, being a central element serving as an ultimate authority), and with its theme of subjective adherence, a believing, required implicitly or through an invitation to be accepted (the moment when a human subject responds to what is at stake).

Therefore, the religious or something similar exists in worlds where the question of God (whatever form he may take) is not raised and where believing (again whatever form that may take) is not brought up, either. Therefore, theology, as an act or posture, appears to be related to a particular way of situating oneself in the world and perceiving humans within it. Referring to transcendence, it is

---

[6] For example, S. Mancini, "Logique des fondements et logique orthopratique. Le problème théologique de la croyance à l'épreuve du culte populaire des images habillées au Mexique", in J. Ehrenfreund/P. Gisel (dir.), *Mises en scène de l'humain. Sciences des religions, philosophie, théologie* (Paris: Beauchesne, 2014) 93–110.

then at best *one* way among others of responding to what, at the very heart of the world, exceeds what is human or overwhelms it, and this way may be subjected to criticism. It is, in fact, criticised today for being anthropocentric, reduced to humans and what they appropriate, and for the imperialistic preference given to reason and intelligibility.

This criticism is becoming more insistent as our (post-modern) era seems to be emerging from its defined orbit, marked by a return to transcendence and the arrival centre-stage of a human subject who is accountable to himself and the world.[7] We are, in fact, witnessing today various options for a spirituality without God or secular spirituality (which is significantly referred to as spirituality rather than religion),[8] against a backdrop that talks of life-balance and wisdom, along with the implementation of personal development, connected to cosmic energy, rather than related to something transcendent which is understood as other, a disturbing reality, and claiming something.

Beyond these indications coming from anthropology and the changes at work at the heart of contemporary life, it is the very definition of what is meant by religion which

---

[7] An era of a "heroic" type of posture, as Charles Taylor expresses well in *A Secular Age* (Cambridge, Mass.: Harvard University Press, 2007), linked to "mobilisation", as Peter Sloterdijk would say, cf. *La mobilisation infinie* (Paris: Bourgois, 2000 [original: *Eurotaoismus*, 1989]).

[8] See A. Comte-Sponville, *L'Esprit de l'athéisme. Introduction à une spiritualité sans Dieu* (Paris: Albin Michel, 2006); L. Ferry, *La Révolution de l'amour. Pour une spiritualité laïque* (Paris: Plon, 2010); R. Dworkin, *Religion Without God* (Cambridge, Mass.: Harvard University Press, 2013).

is becoming porous or which is disintegrating. What I have referred to elsewhere as "vague religions" (*religieux diffus*) – movements such as New Age – has already shown this to be true.⁹

We are therefore led to consider a perspective which is not cantered on religion, however diverse its expressions may be, a perspective which, rather, is displacing it and inscribing it in a larger scheme – that of apparatuses that define culture and society and dictate the status and function of religion, apparatuses that are historically changing.¹⁰ Herein lies the fundamental reason which prevents this work from simply being organised around several traditions (multi-confessionalism) and also prohibits the construction of an intellectual place for questions which would be religious in nature, and according to which, various religious crystallisations and their rearrangement could be studied.

Concretely, it is possible on the contrary, to consider a perspective which is ordered around a religious scene – a changing scene – where the social and anthropological issues of which it is symptomatic may be heard.¹¹

---

⁹ Cf. my booklet *Qu'est-ce qu'une religion* (Paris: Vrin, 2007).
¹⁰ The word 'apparatus' refers to Michel Foucault, cf. P. Veyne, *Michel Foucault. His Thought, His Character* (Cambridge, UK: Polity Press, 2010), which refers to G. Agamben, *What is an Apparatus?* (Redwood City: Stanford University Press, 2009).
¹¹ For further reading, see my submission "El estatus y la función de lo religioso en la Academia como debate social: Visión desde la Universidad", *Teología y Vida* 57, 4 (2016) 539–558.

Consequently, this study of religion – whatever its kind – hinges on civil society and the pluralities that traverse it, a society which is now viewed as a third party, to which can be added a consideration of politics in particular, that is to say, the state and its secularism (the state as arbiter *and* also careful to favour the expression of differences internal to civil life, opposed to all homogenisation and unidimensionality). Here, civil society is a necessary third party, preventing as much a potential focus on religion alone as a face-to-face between religion and what could be a substitute for it of the same level and function (such as a form of the state, or a particular institution of civil society).

4. *For a Genealogical Approach to the Questions Related to Defining the Issues*

The opening point in the preceding section alluded to this: when studying religion and defining the issues, it is necessary to approach it from an historical perspective, of long duration, which includes a comparison of the areas of civilisation. The apparatuses which place demands on the religious, or on what can be termed as such, are not the same in Greco-Roman antiquity (see the works of Jean-Pierre Vernant, Marcel Detienne or John Sheid) as in what has come to make up the main tradition of the West, in India or in China, for example.

We shall now proceed to a genealogical reading (within which the issues to be studied will be placed), which will reveal the various implementations allowing us to define the issues, or indeed outline the typologies. Among these issues, immediately centrally important to the 'Where do we come from?' and the 'How we get out of it and for what?' (which in turn raises the question of the present), can also be mentioned: what is to be understood by religion; the question of God, of transcendence or of what exceeds us; what of believing and, related to this, the question of the human subject, within each case, their diversities and shifts.[12]

To my mind, such a genealogical perspective, with its accompanying issues (on the backdrop to a story involving the advent of humans, and therefore of instincts or desires to be expressed and validated, hinging on specific motives, the whole being based on a present reality and its overlying problems or aporia, to be exposed and diagnosed in turn) is necessary, whether it be in theology, religious studies or cultural and social philosophy.

Setting up the proposed genealogical perspective pre-supposes that it be articulated to, and correlated with, culture and society itself, rather than to some tradition or other. Having said this, traditions have given, and continue to give, shape to what is at stake in each of the issues to be studied and elaborated. Their context cannot be glossed over, all the more so as these issues can only be dealt with through specific, historically situated approaches which

---

[12] Slavoj Žižek seems to me to be typical in this, as is Peter Sloterdijk, both of them on the joint question of God and the human subject.

account for these issues, engaging in a process of honest adherence and a way of building identity beyond the actual discontinuities.

This leads to the implementation of two models, with a form of compatibility to be considered, but without homogenisation. Institutionally, religion cannot be defended today without faculties or other types of academic platforms being considered, reconsidered or established according to a tradition, on the one hand, or according to the global religious scene, on the other; several traditions are to be found on the global religious scene, along with other things which do not pertain to traditions, and various connections with society itself are played out here. The former group integrate into their work the question of which form can, and should, be given to their tradition in a new context or present reality. (It is not the institutions organised around the global religious scene which dictate how Christianity or Islam should, or could, be today in various places, although their work can be indirectly useful to a process of reflection carrying and carried by a tradition.) However, while tied to a tradition, these faculties or academic institutions are at the same time useful to society: it is in fact beneficial to all, indirectly, if a tradition studies its history and present reality. While it is part of society's global intellectual responsibility to nourish institutions that teach and research religious issues (since these issues are relevant to and affect society), without simply leaving them to the traditions which support them (which should be examined in an decentred way), it is also in the interest of all that there be Islamic, Christian and other faculties, and it may even be advisable to encourage their development.[13]

5. *For a Productive Coexistence of Theology and Religious Studies*

Religious studies are rich in the knowledge of humans as they relate to the world, to themselves and to what is beyond them. This knowledge has been forged through a huge variety of apparatuses and organisations which have led to the occupation of space and time; symbolisations of society; rituality; the implementation of references, memories and traditions; ways of perceiving institutional issues, with their various powers and authorities, their modifications and the moments of dissidence and utopia that traverse them, as well as creative representations which orient, define, open up and condition life.

Religious studies are diverse. Religious studies are not singular, but involve an array of other disciplines such as history, anthropology, sociology, psychology and even more regulatory disciplines (religion is laden with regulation): law, political science, philosophy and medicine, among others. It is not one discipline, but an array of disciplines, ultimately because the religious or religion is not

---

[13] On this topic, cf. my submission, "Une double vocation de la théologie, interne et externe. Ordres différents et compatibilité", *Études théologiques et religieuses* 88, 3 (2013) 375-390.

in and of itself an object requiring a particular approach or method of study. The matter of religion is, on the contrary, open-ended and cannot be resolved apart from the accompanying issues, and therefore in isolation from cross-cutting questions. There exists a scanty but significant history of the study of religions (in modern times, in about the last 150 years), and this history has revealed a set of issues which, as such, have created a well-defined field of study, including the fact that these issues have been raised, approached and thought through in ways which are diverse, contradictory and at times even polemical.

Note that the same is true of theology, which is also linked today to diverse fields of historical and social knowledge. That which is by nature theological cuts across what unfolds and is observable in each of the studied fields (specifically: knowledge of the Bible and its contexts; the history of Christianity, with its various productions, including doctrines; the current situation and events; etcetera), and hence second, it is fundamentally problematising and reflexive. Here, too, we see a history of diversified development: that of theology, including as far as status is concerned, a history that is instructive both in and of itself and in terms of what is at stake.

Religions are always diverse and particular. Even their claims to be universal (when they have them, which is not always the case) are determined by a particular perspective. A theology will never go beyond these particularities, unless it considers one religion as the only true one, true in its very particularity or positivity (which it can be tempted to do, but to its own loss, becoming pure ideologisation and idolatry). At best, and this is key, it might succeed in making its particularities productive[14] through their historicisation and the possible resulting shifts and confrontations.

Apart from the illusion of universalistic reason (an illusion which, in modern times, has taken on the form of a theory of progress, from animism to polytheism, then to monotheism, even at times on to metaphysics and ultimately science), religious studies do not have what it takes to go beyond the diversity and particularities of religions, either, unless religious studies consider it possible to define their object, that is the religious (even though this is a field of questions, albeit expressed in examinable specificities), and to offer *the* knowledge of this field. (There is a plurality of things which are known; they are, moreover, partial, and irreducibly so, because they are tied to diverse points of view, each one being relevant in principle.)

Not unrelated to this, the religious field is shot through with traditions, and some, on the part of theologians, have been tempted to select one of them as the right one, or to think they should all be studied and inhabited in juxtaposition, against a backdrop of tolerance, but with no other benefit. On the other hand, others, on the part of religious studies, find it difficult to consider this reality.

---

[14] For further reading, cf. my farewell lesson, "Résistances des particularités et pièges de l'universel. Pour un usage subversif des corps, des traditions et des frontières", in J. Ehrenfreund/P. Gisel (dir.), *Mises en scène de l'humain* (Paris: Beauchesne, 2014) 227–247.

Pierre Gisel

On the pretext that traditions are responses, building an identity that transcends the actual discontinuities (which is undeniable), in practice the meaning of these traditions is willingly glossed over and the quest to understand them is left out. The reality of building identity is reduced to being merely ideological, although such a construct is central to humanity and society, and it thus remains unable to think through the historical shifts as well as what has always been conceived and developed anew through them. For example, Christianity or Islam are no longer studied or researched as such, but rather *christianities* or *islams*, each reported to a particular time or place. Any other position, so it is thought, leads only to essentialism.[15]

a) Once Again: on Theology
Taking religious studies and what they make manifest into consideration is of great benefit to theological study, primarily because it places theology within a broader context and thus affords the possibility of considering what type of religion the tradition is – let us suppose Christianity – which theology seeks to account for, with its own strengths and risks, strengths and risks which are related to its own particular way of shaping general and open human dispositions.

More broadly, entering the area which is examined by religious studies allows theology to unfold a part of what has been known in Catholic terminology, since the middle

---

[15] I recently covered this theme in *Qu'est-ce qu'une tradition? Ce dont elle répond, son usage, sa pertinence* (Paris: Hermann, 2017).

of the twentieth century, as fundamental theology, to differentiate it from dogmatic theology. The area in question is therefore analogous to what metaphysics brought in the thirteenth century, for example, or what the philosophical theologies, which developed theodicies, brought in the seventeenth century.

On the level of the elements specific to the tradition which is being considered (pertaining to dogmatic theology rather than to fundamental theology), taking religious studies into consideration will foster an examination of each concrete proposition – symbolic, ritual, doctrinal, institutional or other – within that tradition, highlighting the human realities to which they answer in every instance. None of these propositions can indeed be considered in and of itself a salvation good, referring to extrinsicism, and consequently not without a self-referencing network. Presuming the opposite would be to sign away the possibility of attributing intelligence to these propositions and would also presuppose a literally alienating religious or belief system. Any affirmation or set up of believing elements is a way of responding to wider human issues and dealing with them on that level,[16] understanding them consequently presupposes examining them from this perspective, and on the basis of a plurality which allows them to be outlined and evaluated.

---

[16] Cf. my *Du religieux, du théologique et du social. Traversées et déplacement* (Paris: Cerf, 2012), 103f, 107; along with my remarks referring to a part of the work of a "fundamental theology".

In all this, a productivity related to frequenting the field of religious studies nourishes theology's own work and reflection, and this will be to its own internal benefit.

b) Once Again: on Religious Studies
For religious studies, the benefit of a meeting or connections with theology is indirect, but not marginal or optional, just as the benefit of work in the area of religious studies was indirect for theology, all the while touching the heart of its mission.

Theology is linked to a tradition which ensures, among other things, a part of its regulation, including its responses to the challenges of the time, and its avatars too, all of which has much to teach, in the flux of historical interruptions and today in the midst of secularisation and other social and religious reshapings. Theology, moreover, unfolds as a way of developing the reflective process, thus as an instructive object of observation. Indeed, there is no reason why religious studies should only choose, as the object of study and research, rites, institutional developments and symbolisations, and not theology as such, in its diverse dimensions – theology is an active player in religion, and human elements are formed there just as in any other religious reality.

Beyond this, it seems to me that there are often blind spots on the part of religious studies. This is probably related to the modern history of its formation and the phenomenon of emancipation which I mentioned at the beginning. What I noted earlier regarding the phenomenon of tradition is typical here. In the same way, in religious studies, the question of the canon of Scripture is deliberately put aside, in order to study all texts, canonical and apocryphal, on an even footing. This is a legitimate way of operating, and it is beneficial on one level (the nature of that benefit ought, however, to be clarified), but it must not lead to pure and simple abandonment: a tradition needs canonisation processes (furthermore, such processes are a human and social phenomenon which go beyond the religious field, even if it is particularly visible in this field), and the way in which a tradition has made its choices and what it has chosen contributes to its very make-up today.

The same can be said concerning doctrinal matters. Here again, as with the canonisation of normative texts, this aspect should not be excluded (nor should it be relegated to theology alone). Furthermore, the fact that theology has already done a work which can be seen as mediating or assimilating can only serve to facilitate an understanding (even if everything must be translated or transposed) of what a tradition has to offer, what is at play or at stake. For example: a traditional reflection on non-duality is taken into account in understanding Buddhism, but the same will also need to be true of Christian theology's reflection on the notion of principle (a central and socio-cultural issue widely shared at the heart of late Antiquity), with the goal of giving it a specific status and function through considering it as *one*, without necessarily considering it to be *simple* (the principle may be relevant to the determination and to an effectuation, not only to the source, which is ensured by the Trinitarian view of

God thus engaged.) The same is also true – the list of examples could be long – of Christological considerations, which are a way of clarifying the issue of mediation (once again a broad issue and, as a matter of fact, an issue which is decisive, at the heart of contemporary society and closely connected to what is happening to its institutions) and of giving it a form of status (an intermediary status? As third party?[17] Other?).

In section four, I defended the importance of a genealogical account in relation to defining a problematology, and while this is, as I see it, necessary for all, theology is more readily inclined than religious studies to move in this direction. Why? Probably because theology cannot exist without a historical awareness which encompasses long eras of history, and consequently theology casts doubt on both breaking it into successive periods (periods, which, moreover, are severed from questions which may connect these periods), and the tendency to focus on what is here merely understood as fact – this or that isolated event, this or that particular person, this or that time of a text's production, etcetera. What a tradition or society makes of a particular event or figure or text, along with its way of relating to them, is decisive; it makes history and belongs precisely within the field of history, which is not merely an accumulation of events or the production of possible references.

---

[17] On the status of third party in this context, refer to my "Réponse à Silvia Mancini", in Ehrenfreund/Gisel (dir.), *Mises en scène de l'humain*, 111–133, on pp. 121–124.

Ultimately, there is an appeal to be made in the face of a neutralising trend present at the heart of religious studies, a neutralising trend which is probably related to wider contemporary socio-cultural elements. Beyond its innate attachment to long duration and problematisation, theology has the vocation to validation of heresy (this is not as true of religious studies, to the extent that it means to unfold independently of normative aspects), and primarily because it carries the issue of what is heterogeneous and what is probably needed to develop in the direction of the heterological.[18]

Venturing into theology's themes and area of reflection can only be beneficial for religious studies, even if, here too, the benefits are indirect (as is the case for theology, as I stated above), since things must be transposed and translated into their own, proper place. This venturing into the theological field represents an enrichment in terms of the elements to be considered, and it may also lead to a revisiting of basic questions to be explored, humanly and socially.

---

[18] This term refers to what Michel Foucault discusses, cf. particularly *Le Corps Utopique, suivi de Les Hétérotopies* (Paris: Lignes, 2009). It remains to consider the outworking of this social heterotopia of all and to show how it can be fruitful and not provide a pretext for sectarianism: cf. on this topic my text, "Défis actuels: Quel profil et quel service pour l'Église dans la société contemporaine?", *Positions luthériennes* 64, 1 (2016) 59–75.

The Changing Soul of Europe: The Challenge to the Secular State
Enzo Pace

1. *Introduction*

Those who are travelling from the heart of the Po Valley in Italy to the Midlands in Britain, from Germany to the Netherlands, from al-Andalus to the Enchanted Moorish Land in Portugal, would not be struck by any places of worship that appear different from those most familiar, such as churches with their bell towers or gold domes. It would not be noticeable, to the naked eye, how the religious landscape in Europe is now being populated with numerous new temples. Some tourist companies will update the traveller online with a new socio-religious map of Europe. Only on arriving in Britain would they finally realise how many mandir (Hindu temples), gurudwara (Sikh temples), Shia, Sunna and Ahmadiyya mosques have been built next to a church (Anglican or Catholic or Methodist), according to the classic canons of the sacred architecture of these various buildings. In addition, many meditation centres referring to various Buddhist schools (dharma) have multiplied. We are facing an unprecedented European religious diversity.

This produces unexpected effects in the other spheres of social life: on education, hospitals, social services and prisons as well as on urban plans for the destination of the areas to be used for new places of worship. Moreover, it is not merely by chance that for several years now in continental European countries, which experienced the first wave of migration that began immediately after the construction of the Berlin Wall in 1961, places of prayer shared by many religions have been inaugurated. There are, for instance, silence rooms in some hospitals and hospices having no particular confessional reference. In many cases, interfaith spaces have opened and function in international airports or in cities. One example of these is the Kamppi Chapel of Silence in the central Norinkka Square in Helsinki, constructed entirely of wood in the shape of a ship, designed in 2012 by the department of social services. Another is the Haus der Religionen in Bern, which since 2002 has hosted two Christian places of worship, a Muslim prayer centre, a small Hindu temple, a Buddhist meditation centre, a space reserved for Jews and another for the followers of the Baha'i faith. Finally, albeit different from the above-mentioned examples, there is the multi-cultural and multi-cult neighbourhood (called the *Esplanade des réligions*), which was completed between 2012 and 2014 by the mayor of the city of Bussy-Saint-George en Seine et Marne. Here, we can find two Buddhist temples, a mosque, a synagogue, a Chinese evangelical church and an Armenian cultural and religious centre, as well as a Catholic church. Moreover, according to the studies by Dionigi Albera on shared sacred space and the revival of pilgrims' paths in Europe,[1] I can recall the attendance at the shrine of the Saint Rosalia by the Tamil community in Palermo,[2] or the same community that returns on 1 May every year to St Anthony church in Padova.

From a socio-religious point of view, Europe is therefore an open construction site. Millions of women and men who live there have been unable to share its long cultural and religious history. Over the lines and fractures that the compass of Christianity has traced on the map of Europe, in a short period of time other lines have been superimposed. They are like points generating other world-religions, or new global Pentecostalism. The conflicts of European religious memory have been partly reduced, for example those generated by the clash between Roman Catholicism and the Reformation. At the same time, negative anti-Semitic stereotypes continue to reappear, a sign of the difficulty of tackling what constitutes Europeans' great cultural and religious remorse, the Shoa.

In the political repertoire and rhetoric of the European ethno-nationalist parties, which tend to stigmatise Islam as the only true enemy of European civilisation, the reference to the defence of Christian identity sounds

---

[1] J. Eade/D. Albera (ed.), *International Perspectives on Pilgrimage Studies* (London: Routledge, 2015).
[2] C. Natali/G. Burgio, "I Tamil in Emilia Romagna e Sicilia", in E. Pace (ed.), *Le religioni nell'Italia che cambia* (Rome: Carocci, 2013) 201–214.

ambiguous: the Christianity they are talking about is actually the symbolic code that reveals the ideological drive towards the ethnic cleansing of one particular idea of Europe, which to their eyes appears decadent, contaminated by barbarous, alien and dangerous religions. It is a sign of the growing difficulty, on the part of a large number of Europeans, to accept that religious diversity, in any case, challenges the secular state, even though we have seen a great variety of models of the secular state.[3]

The new historical phase is characterised by the passage from a pluralism of tolerance, with a progressive low tension between macro belief systems that influenced the European collective consciousness (Christianity in all its various configurations and Judaism), towards interactive pluralism. Even more with the passing of generations, for the women and men of European citizenship who will have to learn to live under the same roof, the interactive pluralism implies the question of the recognition of differences. It will be a question of changing our point of view since we cannot continue to speak of *us* and *them*: the socio-religious morphology is plural, represented by many different religious experiences and practices.

---

[3] H. Vilaça/E. Pace/l. Furseth/P. Pettersson (ed.), *The Changing Soul of Europe: Religions and Migrations in Northern and Southern Europe* (London: Routledge, 2014).

2. Visible Religious Diversity: Gurudwara, Mandir, Mosques, Orthodox Parishes, Buddhist Pagodas, Neo-Pentecostal African Churches

All the greatest world-religions and the minority movements that have developed within them, or have broken away from them, are found today in Europe, as are the avant-gardes of new religions and new churches that were founded in the southern hemisphere of the world. The latter are an expression of neo-Pentecostal Christianity that, at least since 1980, has emerged, respectively, in various countries of sub-Saharan Africa, Latin America and Asia. In societies with increasingly visible religious diversity, symbolic conflicts are partly unexpected. These conflicts are signs of a profound change that is taking place in the innermost folds of almost all European societies. It is the memory, the collective identity and the equality before the law that are concerned.

Moreover, in religions the eye plays an important role. As long as the eye is lazily accustomed to reflecting the images it sees around itself, it refers clearly to the mind the idea that the religious symbols we see are part of our daily life. These symbols represent a thousand-year history, interpret a common feeling (believe it or not), recognise each other in whole or in part and constitute a taken-for-granted, meaningful horizon for everyday life. When other symbols of other religions begin to become visible, the image that we have constructed of a religion familiar to the eye is no longer as reassuring as before. We are forced to focus on other symbols: some may disturb us more than they disturb others, which means that the reaction and adaptation of the eye to new symbols that are, at times, perceived as foreign and threatening, are much slower than the change that, in the meantime, has already taken place in social reality. Adaptation is on average slower than the pace of socio-religious change, which reminds me of the paradox of Zeno of Elea concerning Achilles and the tortoise. The paradox tells us that society follows two different speeds, that of Achilles and that of the turtle. The former is certain to win the race against time, while the latter moves slowly, seemingly unable to beat the former. Achilles, as the paradox says, cannot reach the slow animal because the turtle is the future while the heroic and legendary warrior, who proudly thinks he is invincible, is the past. He tends to look back at the mythical moment when his mother made him invincible and almost invulnerable (except for his heel, as we know), by immerging him in the sacred river Styx.

In absence of systematic studies and reliable sources concerning the quantitative dimensions of this transformation occurring under the sacred canopy of religions, a good preliminary exercise for the socio-optics of religious diversity is precisely the map of places of worship.

It is not easy to see a gurudwara, a Sikh temple, unless you are in Britain, where people from Punjab have been arriving since 1854 thanks to the colonial ties of the British Commonwealth. The population of Punjabi origin and of Sikh faith has become, over the generations, about six hundred thousand. There are 177 temples throughout the country, including Northern Ireland. Many of these temples are clearly visible, such as those in Southall (West London) and Gravesend (Kent). The latter, which cost more than twenty million dollars, is one of the largest with a prayer hall that can accommodate over three thousand people. If the eye of a British person has become accustomed to focusing on the signs of the presence of Sikhs, who are to be found in Bradford or Birmingham as well as in London or Cardiff, it is not so easy for those who live in the Old Continent. Their visibility is still scarce, with the exception of some areas in Northern Italy. In actual fact, Italy hosts the largest Sikh community in Europe, second only to the UK. There are about ninety thousand Sikhs here, according to the cross estimates of the latest migration report,[4] and residency permits issued by the Ministry of the Interior, concentrated above all in the Po Valley or in the valleys with a high level of industrialisation that stretch from the Brescia area to the Pordenone hinterland. Their activity ranges from the breeding of livestock – the first ring in the Italian agro-food industry – to the manufacturing sectors. Then there are 70 Hinduist mandir (temples), which are most widespread in the UK, Germany and Switzerland.

To move on from Sikh and Hindu temples to mosques, the Muslim religious landscape in Europe is far more densely punctuated by mosques and prayer centres

---

[4] D. Denti/M. Ferrari/F. Perocco (ed.), *I Sikh. Storia e immigrazione* (Milan: FrancoAngeli, 2005); B. Bertolani, "I Sikh", in Pace (ed.), *Le religioni nell'Italia che cambia*, 31–46.

(musallayat), the former clearly in greater number than the latter. There are still only a few mosques built according to Muslim sacred architecture to be seen. In all, there are 8,102 Muslim places of worship places.[5] At the top of the list of countries with the highest number of mosques and musallyat, we find Germany (2,600), France (2,100), United Kingdom (1,200), Italy (784) and The Netherlands (430).

From 2000 to 2017, the number of Orthodox parishes increased significantly. In seventeen years, the new ones constitute 70% of the total 1,236 parish units, according to data provided by the Orthodox World Directory. In an ideal ranking of countries, where parishes are active, in first place we find Italy (355), followed by Germany (334), France (240), Great Britain (217), Spain (79), Belgium (53) and the Netherlands (45). Other countries such as Austria (12), Sweden (9), Ireland (5), Portugal (2) and San Marino (1) follow with significantly lower numbers. In this classification, there are also those countries in the European Union that historically have Orthodox minorities, such as Finland, the Czech Republic and Slovakia (with an autocephalous church), Poland and Hungary.

The fact is that the presence of Orthodox parishes is becoming consolidated, with a first generation of 'popes'. On average, they are younger than the Catholic priests and Protestant pastors, were formed in their countries of origin and are, for the time being mainly housed in Catholic

---

[5] S. Allievi, *Conflicts over Mosques in Europe* (London: Alliance Publishing Trust, 2009).

Churches granted by bishops to the various local Orthodox communities.

It is not easy to estimate how many people today are frequent visitors to the various Buddhist centres scattered throughout Europe: ranging from 0.6% to 0.5% of the population, in Norway and France respectively. In the other European countries, the number is close to 0.3%, about three million people.[6] Among Europeans, there are those who come from countries with a majority of Buddhists and follow the teachings of the different schools that established themselves in the past and in modern times, including those that have been labelled as neo-Buddhist, which have often spread from Japan to the West. The best known case is that of the Soka Gakkai (Society for the Creation of Value), which is widespread in twenty European countries; in Italy there are more than fifty thousand followers, and a new headquarters was inaugurated in 2014 in Corsico, Milan.

The Diamond Way Buddhism federation, in the 687 centres spread throughout the world, has 455 only in Europe, with the highest peaks in Germany (151), Poland (71), the Czech Republic (60) and Spain (20). The community network was created by two Danes, Hannah and Ole Nydhal, who became Buddhist masters under the guidance of a head of the current Vajrayana (diamond) school that has its roots in Tibet. There are many others federations of

---

[6] L. Obadia (ed.), "Le Bouddhisme en Occident: Approches sociologique et antropologique", *Recherches Sociologiques* 31, 3 (2000).

similar centres, at least a dozen, to mention only the best known and structured. For example, The Foundation of Preservation of the Mahayana Tradition, with 68 centres in Europe, or the Bodhi Path Centres (with 25 centres, almost half of which are in Germany), or the network of 36 sôtô-sen monasteries in France (11), Germany (7), Italy (7), Switzerland (6), Spain (2), Norway, the Netherlands and Poland (with one centre each). In France, the Village des Pruniers in Dordogne is very well known. Here, a monk of Vietnamese origin gathered around him thousands of followers and sympathisers for many years.[7] We must not forget, either, what is happening in a Catholic monastic environment, where some Benedictines or Dominicans have learned some of the many forms of meditation proposed by Buddhist schools and grafted them onto Christian spirituality. One significant example is that of Father Willigis Jäger (born in 1925), a German Benedictine monk who has in the meantime also become a Zen master.

3. *The Growing SBNR (Spiritual But Not Religious People)*

According to a study conducted by the Pew Research Center (2012),[8] the number of Americans who do not identify

---

[7] J. Zhe, *Religion, modernité et temporalité: une sociologie du bouddhisme chan contemporain* (Paris: CNRS Editions, 2016).

[8] Pew Research Center, "The Spiritual but not Religious" (Washington D.C 2012), http://www.pewforum.org/religious-landscape-study/religious-denomination/spiritual-but-not-religious/, 17 July 2018.

with any religion increased from 15% in 2007 to 20% in 2012, and this number continues to grow. One fifth of US citizens, and a third of adults under the age of 30, are reportedly unaffiliated with any religion. However, they identify themselves as being spiritual in some way. According to recent survey and qualitative researches,[9] a percentage on average of about 30% of Europeans feel that they stand, from a religious point of view, on a middle ground, which is partly unknown and partly already tilled by the baby-boomer generation.

We can use the formula of post-secular, a relatively new cognitive and emotional map that orients people in a socio-religious environment that is changing sharply, to outline not the de-secularisation process according to the last Peter Berger's (1929–2017) report,[10] but the late effects of secularisation. Post-secular actually can bridge the gap between the secular and the religious world-views.

We can draw much empirical evidence from surveys focusing particularly on the new generation's attitudes and behaviour in the religious field. They are experiencing

---

[9] Cf. J. Casanova, *Public Religion in Modern World* (Chicago: University of Chicago Press, 1994); P. Helaas/L. Woodhead, *The Spiritual Revolution* (Oxford: Oxford University Press, 2006); N. Göle, *Islam and Public Controversy in Europe* (London: Routledge, 2014); J. Stolz et al., *(Un)Believing in Modern Society* (London: Routledge, 2016); L. Woodhead, *That was the Church, that was* (London: Bloomsbury Continuum, 2016); P. Bréchon/F. Gauthier, *European Values. Trend and Divides over Thirty Years* (Leiden: Brill, 2017).

[10] P. Berger, *The Many Altars of Modernity: Toward a Paradigm for Religion in a Pluralist Age* (Boston/Berlin: De Gruyter, 2014).

a peculiar condition of (not religious but spiritual) *none*. The signs and symbols of the religions of one's birth are no longer the standpoint from which to challenge the religion of one's fathers and mothers. This means believing in a more open and critical way but still within the framework of beliefs received, or, alternatively, not believing and no longer feeling part of a church or religious tradition, while still declaring oneself to be seeking or interested in inner debate,[11] or, again, having other religious experiences or, finally, adopting one's own, since the received signs and symbols no longer speak to one's conscience.

Post-secular in this sense is not only an interpretative category proposed in particular by Jürgen Habermas[12] but also an emerging category of the spirit.[13] It is not only the search for an ethical agreement between believers and non-believers, each one attentive to recognising the other's point of view in the public sphere, in this way according to historical religions an eminent place at the table of the public discussion on the foundations and the reasons for social cohesion or social ties. We can, however, also hear the resonance of a clash not of civilization but of

---

[11] M. Archer, *The Reflexive Imperative in Late Modernity* (Cambridge: Cambridge University Press, 2012).

[12] J. Habermas, "Religion in the Public Sphere", *European Journal of Philosophy* 14, 1 (2006) 1–25; J. Habermas, *An Awareness of What Is Missing: Faith and Reason in a Post-Secular Age* (Cambridge: Cambridge Polity Press, 2011).

[13] M. Rosati, *The Making of a Post-Secular Society* (London: Routledge, 2015).

truth, one armed against the other. Post-secular, on the other hand, is a modern way of no longer believing in the absolute truth, but in the idea that each point of view has its own truth: even when I feel I am in the right (in terms of religious belief), I know that I stand in a position where other faiths may establish themselves and make themselves visible.

Consequently, the various models of secular state that Europe experienced in its early modern history, accompanying the first industrial and the bourgeois revolutions, do not exist. Actually, there are multiple models of the secular state. Jean Baubérot[14] who devoted his studies to the French model, argues that in France there was no unique model of *laïcité*, either, but many attempts to adjust the utopia of the definitive separation between church and state. The ideal of a rigorous non-confessional state and the privatisation of religion is challenged by a double historical-cultural contingency. We can see, on the one hand, societies that are becoming increasingly religiously different and in which religious communities demand to be recognised as public actors, and, on the other, the emergence of forms of post-secular belief, or the awareness that living in a secular way can no longer rely on the certainty of decline and the eclipse of religion from social life.

In the language of social systems theory, the secular state is a system that interacts with an environment that has become socio-religiously differentiated, making

---

[14] J. Baubérot, *Histoire de la laïcité en France* (Paris: PUF, 2017).

it difficult to reduce the complexity that functionally allows a system to maintain its internal equilibrium. If the political system of a society were to learn to transfer and transform external differentiation (in the religious field) into internal differentiation, the risks of organisational entropy would be high. The system would have, metaphorically, a nervous breakdown, as already seems to have occurred in an increasing part of European public opinion facing socio-religious change, produced by migratory flows. There is a nervous crisis that is well interpreted by the new political parties that are called neo-populists in the media. In reality, they are ethno-religious movements, which we have already seen in the past and which we had deluded ourselves we would no longer see. They have been furiously resurrected after the great disillusionment following the great aspirations aroused by the fall of the Berlin Wall. They are the symptom of a change considered reversible and which is not accepted. The differences (of some religions) are considered incompatible with the culture and values of European societies.

4. Conclusion

The slow but continuous movement of the turtle has already in fact produced changes both in the collective memory and in the functioning of the political macro-systems (having effects not only on and in the European states but also on the project of European Union). Achilles has discovered he has a weak point.

Aside from the metaphor, Ernst-Wolfgang Böchenförde's paradox[15] seems to me that to interpret the impasse of secularism (in the dual sense of privatisation and individualisation of the forms of religious belief and belonging, and the supremacy of the secular state) in Europe. If the liberal secular state, based on positive law, is based on the normative premises that it alone cannot guarantee, then the problem – the post-modern question – is precisely pertinent to the sources of political legitimacy. As long as a system is autopoietic, able to increase its internal complexity by facing the external differentiation that occurs in the (social) environment, it manages to put in parenthesis (a sort of systemic *epoché* or of the Cartesian provisional moral) the theme of its foundation. When political-religious movements arise (the so-called fundamentalist movements that we have learned to recognise in almost all the great world-religions, including Buddhism) that instead cry out that the king is naked, that the system is not based on unquestionable premise or on a sacred pact, then the secular state risks sacrificing some of its pre-conditions of existence. In fact, in some European countries (particularly those belonging to the Visegrad Group), the ruling class expressed by the new right-wing parties, is practising politics based on the pattern of majority religions versus religious minorities, solidifying in the law any privileges for the former and limitations for

---

[15] E.W. Böchenförde, *La formazione dello Stato come processo di secolarizzazione* (Brescia: Morcelliana, 2006).

the latter. Democratic and liberal societies, moreover, require a minimum of organic solidarity among its citizens. This symbolic device (which concerns the representation of collective consciousness) is threatened by a double contingency: a tetragonal and intransigent secularism, on the one hand, and, on the other, policies of identity that instrumentally mobilise symbols and religious codes to erect new ideological walls.

The road traced by Habermas in his dialogue and confrontation with Joseph Ratzinger (2007) at the Catholic Academy of Monaco seems to me a good way to improve the best social practices: to translate distinctive signs and symbols of the different religions, present in Europe today, into a universal humanistic language, shared and understandable at the public level. It is an ethical-cultural premise for a new social pact, which implies the self-understanding of every religion as a bearer of truth with limited sovereignty in societies with high socio-religious differentiation. The plurality of faiths can be a normative premise for refining the legitimacy of the post-secular state.

Mutual Recognition in Theology and Modern Society

Risto Saarinen

1. *Current Politics of Recognition*

In his seminal essay of 1992, originally entitled "Multiculturalism and Politics of Recognition", the Canadian philosopher Charles Taylor propels the concept of mutual recognition into contemporary democratic decision-making. While Taylor considers the idea of toleration to be extremely important, he also claims that toleration alone is not sufficient to guarantee the well-being of minorities in democratic societies. Moreover, we need special acts that recognise minorities, and the minorities are supposed to be loyal to the society that recognises them. Through such mutual recognition, the minorities can cherish their cultural difference and at the same time become equal societal partners.[1]

Such acts of recognising others can, at least so the theory says, prevent the segregation of sub-cultures in

---

[1] C. Taylor, "The Politics of Recognition", in his *Philosophical Arguments* (Cambridge, Mass.: Harvard University Press, 1995) 225–256.

multicultural societies. Acts of mutual recognition are expected to prevent the emergence of alternative societies occurring within the macrostructure of democracy. In mutual recognition, majorities identify minorities and affirm their particular identity and right to pursue goals relevant to their own flourishing. In return, the minorities affirm the overall rule of law in the democratic state and commit themselves to cooperate with the society at large.[2]

After Taylor's essay, such politics of recognition, or positive identity politics, has been extensively discussed and debated in social sciences. According to another leading theorist, the German philosopher Axel Honneth, people seek recognition in three distinct and related spheres of life. In the private sphere, people seek loving recognition. As citizens of a democratic state, people seek respect and legal recognition in terms of equality. In their professional life, people seek the esteem that appreciates their individual skills, virtues and goals in life.[3]

According to Honneth, such a broad concept of threefold recognition stems from young Friedrich Hegel's philosophy of *Anerkennung*. From Johann Gottlieb Fichte and Hegel, the concept of recognition already found its way into diplomatic and political theory in the nineteenth century. However, it is only in the late modern identity politics that

---

[2] Cf. S. Thompson, *The Political Theory of Recognition: A Critical Introduction* (Cambridge: Polity, 2006).

[3] A. Honneth, *Kampf um Anerkennung. Zur moralischen Grammatik sozialer Konflikte* (Frankfurt: Suhrkamp, 1992).

the usefulness of mutual recognition as a psychological, social and political concept can be fruitfully understood.[4]

Both Taylor and Honneth consider mutual recognition to be a secular virtue born of the Enlightenment and Hegelian modernity. Recognition is in this way a twin sister to toleration. While toleration provides us with rights permitting freedom, recognition can produce minority rights and social cohesion. Thus the twin sisters contribute to the well-being of late modern, secular, democratic society.[5]

At the same time, Taylor and Honneth also consider that the striving for mutual recognition is a basic psychological and anthropological fact which develops in childhood and concerns all human beings irrespective of particular cultural surroundings. Everyone needs love, respect and esteem everywhere, not just in modern European society or in late modern identity politics. In my view, there is some tension between the alleged emergence of recognition in secular modernity, on the one hand, and the claim of a universal need for recognition, on the other. If people have always strived after recognition, how can it be that this has only been realised since Hegel?

Some philosophers have also enquired into the longer history of recognition discourses. Paul Ricoeur considers that the concept has some roots in the idea of *anagnorisis*,

---

[4] A. Honneth, *The I in We: Studies in the Theory of Recognition* (Cambridge: Polity, 2012), and his *Anerkennung: eine europäische Ideengeschichte* (Berlin: Suhrkamp, 2018).
[5] R. Forst, *Toleranz im Konflikt. Geschichte, Gehalt und Gegenwart eines umstrittenen Begriffs* (Frankfurt: Suhrkamp, 2003).

identification or knowing again, *Wiedererkennen*, a significant theme in Aristotle's poetics. However, Ricoeur also considers that the idea of *Anerkennung*, meaning both identification and normative evaluation, stems solely from Hegel. Ricoeur and his colleague Marcel Hénaff add to this that such recognition may not only emerge from violent struggle but can also be a gesture of hospitality and peaceful exchange of gifts.[6]

Recently, Piero Boitani has published an extensive intellectual history of Aristotelian *anagnorisis*. Boitani points out the Latin terms *agnosco*, *agnitio*, which bring the Aristotelian idea into western literature. It needs to be added, however, that the poetic idea of re-identification is different from the normative recognition outlined by Honneth and Taylor.[7]

This new discussion in social theory has also entered theology. In contemporary German Catholicism, Veronika Hoffmann has investigated its theological potential, in particular when recognition is considered a peaceful exchange of gifts, or a gift of recognition, *eine Gabe der Anerkennung*. In American theology, Timothy Lim has recently published an ecclesiological elaboration of the Hegelian variant.[8]

---

[6] P. Ricoeur, *The Course of Recognition* (Cambridge, Mass.: Harvard University Press, 2005).

[7] P. Boitani, *Riconoscere è un dio. Scene e temi del riconoscimento nella letteratura* (Turin: Einaudi, 2014).

[8] V. Hoffmann, *Skizzen zu einer Theologie der Gabe* (Freiburg: Herder, 2013); T.T.N. Lim, *Ecclesial Recognition with Hegelian Philosophy, Social Psychology and Continental Political Theory* (Leiden: Brill, 2017).

2. Recognition and Religion: Ancient Roots

At the University of Helsinki, we are conducting a research project entitled "Reason and Religious Recognition". Our team includes theologians, historians and philosophers. We are taking the theory of Honneth and Taylor seriously and collaborating with German philosophers and theologians at the universities of Frankfurt and Münster. At the same time, we claim that the history of normative recognition does not start with Hegel but has a long prehistory in Christian theology. As a result of this prehistory, recognition is a far less secular concept than toleration and can be fruitfully applied to ecumenism and other issues of Christian identity. Because this application is genuinely Christian, it does not simply follow Hegel or other modern theories but develops its own theological criteria. In this paper, I shall elucidate this claim of a long Christian history of recognition with some examples.

Let me begin with mentioning three recent publications. A thematic issue of the journal *Open Theology* (2/2016) collects the papers presented at the American Academy of Religion's session on recognition in 2015. The proceedings of Societas Oecumenica, the European university ecumenists' recent conference in Helsinki 2016, is entitled *Recognition and Reception in Ecumenical Relations*.[9]

---

[9] D. Heller/M. Hietamäki (ed.), *Just Do It?! Recognition and Reception in Ecumenical Relations* (Leipzig: Evangelische Verlag, 2018).

My following historical orientations are based on a third publication, namely, my own recent monograph *Recognition and Religion*. In this book, I present my arguments for the claim that recognition is an ancient Christian concept that has influenced modern philosophy but which also has its own, distinct intellectual profile.[10] Like Piero Boitani, I often focus on the Latin terms *agnosco, agnitio*, which since medieval times have been employed as synonymous with *recognosco, recognitio*, and which do not only translate Aristotelian re-identification but are also distinct legal and religious terms.

One point of departure in my own history is the Latin Bible. In the Vulgate, the Greek *ginosko* is normally translated with *cognosco*. The almost synonymous verb *epiginosko* is, however, often translated with *agnosco*. *Agnosco* and *agnitio* are employed in Roman law to highlight some performative legal transactions, such as adoption (*agnitio filii*) and approval of testament (*hereditatem agnoscere*). Due to such performative uses, some passages in the Vulgate give the impression of normative approval due to identification, a meaning that is very close to the idea of recognition.[11]

Influential passages of this kind include 1 Timothy 2:4, reading "God desires everyone to be saved and to come to the knowledge of the truth (*epignosis tes aletheias, agnitio*

---

[10] R. Saarinen, *Recognition and Religion: A Historical and Systematic Study* (Oxford: Oxford University Press, 2016).
[11] Ibid., 42–48.

veritatis). In Titus 1:1, Paul calls himself a servant of God for the sake of the knowledge of truth (again *epignosis tes aletheias*, *agnitio veritatis*). In such passages, the term *agnitio* means not only observation but also approval and affirmation, a performative and normative move which semantically resembles the act of adoption in Roman law.[12]

The phrase *agnitio veritatis* is used prominently in an early Christian novel, the so-called pseudo-Clementine *Recognitions*, of which the Latin translation is extant, and was used throughout the medieval and early modern periods. From the surviving Greek fragments, we know that the word *recognitio* translates the Greek term *anagnorismos*. *Recognitio* and *agnitio* are also used synonymously. The somewhat clumsy plot of this novel reveals a familiarity with the Aristotelian poetic view of re-identification. The novel tells the story of Clement, who meets apostles and his own family members, discovering their identities in the context of his own life story. This horizontal recognition is close to Aristotle's *anagnorisis*.[13]

In addition to this, and most importantly, the novel explains how Clement becomes a true Christian in a vertical encounter with the True Prophet, or God in Jesus Christ. This vertical encounter is repeatedly described using the

---

[12] Ibid., 46–48.

[13] Ibid., 48–54; Clement (pseudo), *Rekognitionen in Rufins Übersetzung* (vol. 2 of B. Rehm/G. Strecker ed., *Die Pseudoklementinen*, Berlin: Akademie-Verlag, 1965); The following translations are from https://en.wikisource.org/wiki/Ante-Nicene_Fathers/Volume_VIII/The_Recognitions_of_Clement, 21 September 2018.

Pauline phrase *agnitio veritatis*. Such *agnitio* is not particularly philosophical but just simple knowledge to modest people:

> For the knowledge of things which is imparted by the true Prophet is simple and plain and brief [...] to modest and simple minds, when they see things come to pass which have been foretold, it is enough, and more than enough, that they may receive most certain knowledge from most certain prescience and for the rest may be at peace, having received most certain knowledge of the truth (*agnitio veritatis*, *Recognitiones* 8, 61:2).

Recognitiones describes the emergence of such knowledge in terms of a struggle in which the mind is illuminated:

> Our mind is subject to errors [...] But the mind has it in its own nature to oppose and fight against these, when the knowledge of truth (*agnitio veritatis*) shines upon it, by which knowledge is imparted fear of judgement to come, which is a fit governor of the mind, and which can recall it from the precipices of lusts (*Recognitiones* 9, 31:2).

In spite of its clumsiness, the pseudo-Clementine *Recognitiones* is a remarkable work since it unites two ancient traditions: recognition, that is, the Aristotelian poetic re-identification, on the one hand, and the legal and Pauline language of vertical *agnitio*, on the other. We find repercussions of this language in Augustine and other Latin patristic sources. Augustine favours the phrases *agnitio*

Dei and *agnitio Christi* but in some cases he may also employ *agnitio veritatis*.[14]

We can thus say that in early Christianity and the Latin patristic era an idea of vertical recognition was already available, an idea that employs views of Aristotelian poetics and Roman law. However, this idea of vertical recognition has its own distinctive content in the act of conversion, in which the mind turns towards the higher truth of revelation, acknowledging its priority vis-à-vis earthly realities. We can label this first Christian idea of recognition as *conversion narrative*, since the *agnitio Christi* or *agnitio veritatis* often means performative metanoia or conversion.

3. *Medieval and Early Modern Recognition Discourses*

In medieval theology, we can see a new vocabulary of mutual recognition emerging. This new vocabulary employs features of feudal law, that is, regulations concerning the relationship between lord and servant. In addition to lord and servant, the loving relationship between bridegroom and bride becomes important. Allegorically, both the lord and the bridegroom can represent God or Christ, while the servant and the bride represent human beings or the faithful. Typically, the lord or the bridegroom in this relationship commends the servant or the bride and gives her a gift, a *beneficium*. The servant or the bride responds

---

[14] Saarinen, *Recognition and Religion*, 54–58.

to this with an act of recognising the lord or the groom. In this description, the Latin verbs *recognosco* and *agnosco* are employed synonymously. They do not signify an act of re-identification but rather an act of normative approval in the mutual bond.

Bernard of Clairvaux's *Sermons on the Song of Songs* frequently use this vocabulary and can be considered a keynote text regarding the medieval view of theological recognition.[15] I shall now, however, resist the temptation to dwell on this wonderful work and proceed straightly to Thomas Aquinas. In Aquinas, we encounter the feudal terminology but also some views which sound astonishingly modern. For instance, Thomas explains the encounter between Mary Magdalene and Christ resurrected as follows: at first, Mary does not identify the other as Christ, but when Christ says to her "Mary", she recognises (*agnovit*) Him. In saying "Mary", Christ is asking her "to recognize him who recognizes you" (*recognosce eum a quo recognosceris*).[16] Significantly, Thomas speaks here of mutual recognition. While the meaning of re-identification is relevant here, the passage probably also includes the idea of mutual affirmation and showing respect.

When Aquinas employs feudal terminology, his conclusions also sound surprisingly modern. He considers that people should react to divine gifts with a proper act taking place *in recognitionem divini beneficii*. He adds that

---

[15] Ibid., 63–69.
[16] Ibid., 69–73. Thomas, *Super Joh.*, 20, lect 3.

such benefit creates a "debt of recognition" (*debitum recognitionis*).[17]

When asked whether we should pay honour to those in positions of dignity, Thomas answers as follows:

> A person in a position of dignity is an object of twofold consideration; first, in so far as he obtains excellence of position, together with a certain power over subjects; secondly, as regards the exercise of his government. In respect of his excellence there is due to him honour, which is the recognition (*recognitio*) of some kind of excellence; and in respect of the exercise of his government, there is due to him worship, consisting in rendering him service [...] repaying him [...] for the benefits we received.[18]

Here, in a seemingly modern fashion, recognition concerns the status of a person, whereas the so-called worship concerns achievements and merits. This sounds somewhat similar to Axel Honneth's distinction between respect and esteem as two basic modes of recognition. The impression is strengthened when Thomas says, in this context, that we owe another person a twofold debt. The so-called legal debt concerns officeholders as pertaining to their status. The so-called moral debt concerns persons without regard to the hierarchies existing between us and them.[19]

---

[17] Thomas, *Summa theol.* II/2, q. 86, a. 4 resp, ad 1.
[18] Thomas, *Summa theol.* II/2, q. 102, a. 2 resp.
[19] Thomas, *Summa theol.* II/2, q. 102, a. 2, ad 2.

While recognition in Thomas Aquinas pertains to normative status and is only very faintly connected to re-identification or memory, it would be misleading to interpret it in a very modern fashion. Thomas assumes the background of feudal law and the exchange between the lord's benefits and the servant's recognition. It is nevertheless striking how mutual this relationship is and that there is a distinction between legal, obligatory respect and more voluntary esteem based on merits and performance. One also needs to remember that the feudal terminology is profoundly relational. We are lords and servants, husbands and wives in a network of mutual dependence. While this relationality is different from late modern constructionism, they both share the idea that our identities are deeply heteronomous. It is this heteronomy and mutual dependence which makes Thomas Aquinas seem modern in many ways.

When we come to the Reformation, the ideas of relational constitution and heteronomy continue to be influential although the feudal law no longer serves as the conceptual background. John Calvin employs recognition terminology repeatedly in his *Institutio*, radicalising many medieval ideas. Calvin teaches that all humans express a sense of natural heteronomy and dependence on some higher being. All people are "compelled to acknowledge (*agnosco*) some God".[20]

This natural heteronomy means not only servanthood but our complete belonging to God, as Calvin formulates in his Puritan manner:

---

[20] J. Calvin, *Inst.* 1, 4, 2. Saarinen, *Recognition and Religion*, 100.

> We are not our own: let neither our reason nor our will, therefore, sway our plans and deeds [...] We are not our own; in so far as we can, let us therefore forget ourselves and all that is ours. Conversely, we are God's; let us therefore live for him and die for him.[21]

Like Thomas Aquinas, Calvin employs recognition terminology in the sense of normative affirmation. For him, however, the event of recognition consists in tribulations and radical self-denial, through which God's true being can be known. I quote:

> In the very harshness of tribulations we must recognize (*recognosco*) the kindness and generosity of our Father towards us [...] When we acknowledge (*agnoscimus*) the Father's rod, is it not our duty to show ourselves obedient and teachable children?[22]

Like the author of Pseudo-Clementine *Recognitiones*, Calvin teaches that we can only recognise God when our confused emotions are set aside, asking rhetorically as follows:

> Where is your recognition of God (*recognitio Dei*) if your flesh boiling over with excessive abundance into vile lusts

---

[21] Calvin, *Inst.* 3, 7, 1. Translations from J. Calvin, *Institutes of the Christian Religion*, ed. by J.T. McNeill (2 vol.; Louisville: Westminster John Knox Press, 2006).
[22] Calvin, *Inst.* 3, 8, 6.

> infects the mind with its impurity [...] Where is our recognition of God (*recognitio Dei*) if our minds be fixed upon the splendour of our apparel? For many so enslave all their senses to delights that the mind lies overwhelmed.[23]

For Calvin, the right knowledge and recognition of God is connected to truthful self-knowledge. Therefore, one must first recognise and confess one's own sinfulness and then look towards God. When this process is successfully completed, Christians can become saints who have true knowledge of God and true self-knowledge. In such a state of clarity, the saints can understand their humanity "without comparison with others, while they recognize themselves before God" (*dum se coram Deo recognoscunt*).[24] In this manner, the absolute dependance on God finally leads to the relative autonomy in which one does not need to compare oneself with other humans.

In this quotation, Calvin uses the reflexive form, *se recognoscere*, to recognise oneself. The reflexive form is used prominently in many texts of the Renaissance and the Reformation. It also appears in Augustine of Hippo. Paul Ricoeur has dedicated particular attention to the phenomenon of recognising oneself. It is one aspect of the classical philosophical theme of knowing oneself. Ricoeur explains the phenomenon with the help of anamnesis, recollection. We recognise ourselves with the help

---

[23] Calvin, *Inst.* 3, 10, 3.
[24] Calvin, *Inst.* 3, 14, 18. Saarinen, *Recognition and Religion*, 105.

of memory.²⁵ When I wake up in the morning, I re-identify my mind and body with the person who is in my memory from yesterday. When this happens every morning, I have an identity which is given from the memory as the recognition of myself.

This explanation is fitting as far as Augustine is concerned. In the Renaissance and the Reformation, however, the reflexive form *se recognoscere* is employed with a different meaning. The Renaissance philosopher Marsilio Ficino teaches in his *De amore* that I can become aware of my own deeper self when I fall in love and when I see the face of my beloved I can recognise my own deeper self.²⁶ In other words, the relational love between myself and my beloved gives me access to my deeper self. Ficino calls this relational access an act of *se recognoscere*.

Basically, Calvin employs the same figure of thought when he declares that the faithful can recognise themselves only when they let themselves be known and defined by God. In this relationship before God, *coram Deo*, the Christian can recognise him/herself. In this manner, the event of recognising oneself is not an act of memory but an act of interpersonal encounter. We can also see this same figure, recognising oneself through the other, in Martin Luther's monastic struggles with understanding

---

[25] Ricoeur, *The Course of Recognition*, 69–148.
[26] Saarinen, *Recognition and Religion*, 79–87; M. Ficino, *Commentarium in convivium Platonis De amore*, ed. by P. Laurens (Paris: Les Belles Lettres, 2002), esp. II, 8 and VI, 6.

God's righteousness. Luther makes frequent use of the terms *agnosco*, *agnitio*. He teaches that many different kinds of human acknowledgement are necessary in order for humans to be able to renounce their own priorities and give priority to God. Only after such renunciation, can God verify and justify the sinful human person, giving him or her deeper identity.[27]

The period from Bernard of Clairvaux to early modernity constitutes the second paradigm of the Christian theology of recognition. While the first paradigm was labelled as conversion narrative, this second paradigm is far more relational and takes place in a deep mutuality between the partners. As the divine commendation and benefit often occurs in terms of promise, it can be aptly summarised with this term. As the human response and new human condition leads to self-preservation, sometimes as a feudal bond, sometimes as justification and salvation, sometimes as a loving relationship, I summarise this response as self-preservation. Therefore, the second paradigm of Christian recognition expresses the promise of self-preservation.

4. Religious Recognition in Modernity

The first and the second paradigms, conversion narrative and promise of self-preservation, occur predominantly in Latin theological writings. When we come to the modern

---

[27] Saarinen, *Recognition and Religion*, 87–98.

age, we must consider the vernacular terminologies in some detail. English terminology is not very complex, as the verbs *acknowledge* and *recognise* carry over the Latin meanings of *agnosco* and *recognosco*. Regarding French terminology, Paul Ricoeur's historical observations are problematic. He considers that the French verb *reconnaître* started to be used in the seventeenth and eighteenth centuries and received its normative meaning in Jean-Jacques Rousseau.[28]

However, the French edition of Calvin's *Institutio*, published in 1560, already frequently uses *reconnaître* and *reconnaissace*, carrying over the normative meaning available in Latin.[29] In my view, both the English and the French terminology display a remarkable continuation with the Latin tradition.

The German terminology is more complicated, as the words *anerkennen* and *Anerkennung* only started to be employed during the last decade of the eighteenth century. Contemporary social philosophy normally assumes that Hegel was the first thinker to give these terms an elaborated philosophical meaning.

However, if we look at German theological texts, we find a tradition which is older than that of Hegel's time. This tradition interacts with Hegelian philosophy but also remains an independent current of thought. The first German theologian to use *Anerkennung* in a prominent

---

[28] Ricoeur, *The Course of Recognition*, 122, 207–208.
[29] Saarinen, *Recognition and Religion*, 98–110.

fashion is the Berlin Neologist Johann Joachim Spalding. In his popular bestseller, *Religion, eine Angelegenheit des Menschen* (1796), *Anerkennung* is a key notion.[30]

In this book, Spalding develops a philosophy of religion which can escape some of the criticism of theological thought presented by Immanuel Kant. Spalding admits that after Kant we may not present dogmatic or confessional religion in a scientific fashion. He argues, however, that an enlightened person realises that he or she lives with the help of two fundamental instincts or feelings, namely, a desire for moral goodness and a desire for personal happiness. In order to live a reasonable life in which these two feelings exist in harmony, a person must in some way affirm a world-ruler (*Weltregierer*) who guarantees the existence of the goals of goodness and happiness. This act of primary affirmation Spalding calls *Anerkennung*. It is less than confession but more than a Kantian theoretical and practical knowledge.[31]

In keeping with this basic idea, Spalding defines religion as "recognition (*Anerkennung*) of the most perfect world-ruler in his relationship to us". This means that the act of recognition does not produce objective knowledge but an affirmation from the first-person stance, a "relationship to us". With the help of this primary *Anerkennung*, the enlightened person can believe in the goodness

---

[30] Ibid., 125–136; J.J. Spalding, *Religion, eine Angelegenheit des Menschen* (Tübingen: Mohr Siebeck, 2001).

[31] Spalding, *Religion, eine Angelegenheit des Menschen*, 24. My translations.

and happiness that is available for him.[32] Spalding thus produces a derivation of many basic issues from the primary act of *Anerkennung*, as follows:

> Finding a harmony between goodness and happiness is only possible through the recognition (*Anerkennung*) of a being that has intentionally equipped the soul with both basic feelings, so that neither of them is there in vain, without expected fulfilment. [...] With this conviction, the virtuous person has much more courage and his prevalence is confirmed. He can then say firmly and confidently: I will be true to my conscience, since through it alone I will in the end obtain everything that is good for me. He who made me will take care of that. But also for this reason I will honour the religion that justifies my saying this.[33]

When Spalding considers the act of *Anerkennung* to be the basic affirmation of a religious world-view, he effects a move which is typical of most modern theories of recognition. In this modern view, the act of recognition produces a change in the object's status. In Spalding, this change in status is not philosophical or political but rather an existential first-person status change. The primary act of recognition affirms the importance of the object for me personally. I call this modern view and third religious paradigm existential status change.

---

[32] Ibid.
[33] Ibid., 32–33.

Spalding is nevertheless traditional in the sense that, for him, it is the human being who recognises the importance of God. This usage is common in both the first paradigm of conversion and the second paradigm of self-preservation. Shortly after Spalding, Friedrich Schleiermacher reverses the order of status change. In his prominent dogmatics, *Der christliche Glaube*, Schleiermacher defines the act of justification as follows:

> That God justifies the person who converts entails that God forgives his sins and recognizes (*anerkennt*) him as a child of God. This change of a person's relationship with God occurs only when he has a true faith in the redeemer.[34]

Schleiermacher here conceives *Anerkennung* as a downward act, through which God justifies the human being. In his commentary on this statement, Schleiermacher reflects on the concept of childhood of God, connecting this theme to adoption and Roman law. Schleiermacher's use of the concept of recognition is not accidental. He connects the downward *Anerkennung* to the ancient legal model of adoption. Like in Spalding, however, it is the status change of the object which is distinctive in the act of religious recognition.

---

[34] F.D.E. Schleiermacher, *Der christliche Glaube nach den Grundsätzen der evangelischen Kirche in Zusammenhange dargestellt. 2nd ed. (1830/31)* (Berlin: De Gruyter, 2003), §109.

The theological view of *Anerkennung* continues from Spalding and Schleiermacher to the dialectical theology of the twentieth century. We find it prominently represented in Rudolf Bultmann's entries to Gerhard Kittel's *Theologisches Wörterbuch des Neuen Testaments*. In both the entry *ginosko*, to know, and *pisteuo*, to believe, Bultmann considers that in the Biblical vocabulary the act of knowing entails the act of affirming or recognising (*anerkennen*). Bultmann says, for instance, that a human understanding of divine will is "primarily recognition, an obedient or thankful submission to what is known". Christian knowledge is "an obedient and grateful recognition (*Anerkennung*) of the deeds and demands of God". Gnosis in the New Testament does not mean theoretical information but a "recognition of God's new plan for salvation". The Greek term *epignosis*, in particular, is "almost a technical term for the decisive knowledge of God which is implied in the conversion to the Christian faith".[35]

It is fascinating that in these words of Bultmann we should hear our first paradigm, the idea that *agnitio veritatis* is basically a conversion. At the same time, we also hear the modern paradigm of existential status change. A Christian does not receive religious information but he or

---

[35] R. Bultmann, *ginosko* and *pisteuo* in G. Kittel (ed.), *Theologisches Wörterbuch zum Neuen Testament* (vol. 1; Stuttgart: Kohlhammer, 1933), 688–719; ibid. (vol. 6; Stuttgart: Kohlhammer, 1959), 174–230; Saarinen, *Recognition and Religion*, 158–161.

she makes a first-person leap into faith, a primary recognition which makes everything else meaningful.

Karl Barth likewise makes use of such a primary and existential understanding of recognition. In his *Kirchliche Dogmatik*, he opposes the idea that religious conviction proceeds from knowledge to assent. In Barth's view, such an order does not pay proper attention to the primacy of assent in religious faith. Like Spalding, Barth teaches that we must first make an act of recognition, *Anerkennen*, in order to make sense of religion. In his view, faith consists in *Anerkennen*, *Erkennen* and *Bekennen*, that is recognition, knowing and confessing, which follow in this order. Barth explains:

> Christian faith is an acknowlegdement, *Anerkennen*. In our description [...] this must come first [...] Knowing, *Erkennen*, is certainly included in the acknowledgement, but it can only follow it. Acknowledgement is a cognition which is obedient and compliant, which yields and subordinates itself. This obedience and compliance is not an incidental and subsequent characteristic of the act of faith, but primary, basic, and decisive. It is not preceded by any other kind of knowledge, either knowing or confessing.[36]

In other words, Barth claims, like Bultmann and Spalding, that the act of recognition must come first in Christian

---

[36] K. Barth, *Kirchliche Dogmatik* (vol. 4/1; München/Zürich: TVZ, 1932–1967), 847–848 (G. Bromiley's translation slightly modified).

faith. Knowing and confessing make sense after the primary act of *Anerkennen*, recognition. We see here again our third paradigm of theological recognition at work. An existential status change of the object must come first in order for intellectual content to be able to follow. This is, in a way, the classical model of *fides quaerens intellectum*. Let it be mentioned that some contemporary philosophical models are fairly close to Barth's model. Axel Honneth, for instance, claims programmatically that recognition precedes cognition. This is already the case in infant psychology because the infant needs an attachment and an object relationship before it can learn and develop cognitively.[37] While the modern theological model of Bultmann and Barth should not be confused with philosophical theories of recognition, they both affirm an idea of existential attachment which is connected to the object's change in status.

In contemporary German theology, Eberhard Jüngel is a prominent representative of such thinking. In his book on justification by faith, first published in 1998, Jüngel writes that "it is essential for people to be recognized. Their personhood depends on it. As human beings, we demand recognition for ourselves. The wish for justification has its source in this basic human need for recognition".[38]

---

[37] A. Honneth, *Reification: A New Look at an Old Idea* (Oxford: Oxford University Press, 2008).
[38] E. Jüngel, *Justification: The Heart of the Christian Faith* (London: T. & T. Clark, 2006), 78.

To summarise my brief outline of the history of religious recognition in Christianity: recognition is an old topic which has been discussed more or less continually from Early Christianity to today. Three basic paradigms can be detected. The oldest paradigm, conversion narrative, focuses on the change in the recognising subject. The second paradigm, dominant from the twelfth to the eighteenth century, emphasises mutual recognition in a relational setting. In this setting, God makes promises and the human being enters a bond which leads to self-preservation. The idea of self-recognition through others also plays a role in this second paradigm. The third paradigm expresses a status change in the recognised object. In religion, however, this is not a political or diplomatic act but a primary existential attachment which opens the recogniser to a new understanding of religion and theology.

I have emphasised that even the third paradigm is older than Hegel's thought, and that Hegel's thinking may be indebted to the second paradigm. The main finding is, however, that recognition is a classical topic in Christian theology. We should be aware, too, that current theories of recognition also affirm the possibility that recognition does not only pertain to the status of its object. It is rather the case that all parties change in the event of recognition. This is particularly visible in those theories in which recognition is understood in terms of gift exchange. Yet even the Hegelian theories of struggle can make the point that this struggle changes everyone, both the recogniser and the recognised. Christian theology has been aware of all these conceptual possibilities. Therefore, one can say that recognition is a less secular idea than toleration and that the so-called politics of recognition has deep Christian roots.

Having said this, it is important to add that religious recognition cannot provide all the answers elaborated in social theory. Taylor and Honneth aim at clarifying how democratic society can affirm both difference and equality at the same time. In democracy, we can affirm both the lasting difference or otherness and the fundamental and practical equality of every member of society. The tradition of religious recognition outlined above makes some important aspects of otherness visible. Bridegroom and bride, lord and servant, God and God's people recognise one another in terms of lasting otherness. Christian theology can consider issues of positive otherness. On the other hand, such relationships are hierarchical and do not propagate equality in the manner of social theory. There is, however, one field of theology in which horizontal forms of mutual recognition among equals are being elaborated. This is ecumenism, the last section in my presentation.

5. Recognition in Ecumenical Theology: Difference and Equality

The concept of mutual recognition among equals was already employed in the early ecumenical movement before the Second World War. That early discussion did not, however, employ a theological concept of recognition.

They rather borrowed the diplomatic concept from international politics. In this manner, a 1937 Faith and Order text formulates as follows:

> To speak of mutual recognition is to enter the area of inter-church relationships. As in the case of civil governments, 'recognition' is a condition or further relationships, so it is with the Churches. Mutual recognition may be partial or complete. It does not necessarily involve any co-operative action or Corporate Union [...].[39]

After the Second World War we notice an elaboration of the idea of mutual recognition in the ecumenical movement. According to the so-called Toronto Declaration of 1950, the churches need not to recognise one another when they are members of the World Council of Churches. However, they must all recognise Jesus Christ as the "Divine Head of the Body". In addition, they need to "recognize in other churches elements of the true Church". Such formulations give the impression of a mediated recognition, in which a third party, Jesus Christ, unites the partners who cannot recognise one another directly. This is already a variant of theological recognition.[40]

---

[39] World Conference on Faith and Order, "The meanings of Unity", Report n.1 prepared by the Commission on the Church's Unity in Life and Worship (Edinburgh, 1937).

[40] Lukas Vischer (ed.), *Documentary History of the Faith and Order Movement 1927–1963* (St Louis: Bethany, 1963), 171–173; Saarinen, *Recognition and Religion*, 175.

The texts of the Vatican Council II mark a new awareness and deeper idea of ecumenical recognition. The council texts often employ the old Latin notion of *agnosco* in significant places. *Lumen gentium* (9) considers that God gathers God's people among those who "acknowledge him in truth". *Nostra aetate* (2) speaks of the "acknowledgement of a supreme deity or even of a Father" by the adherents of other religions.

The Decree on Ecumenism, *Unitatis redintegratio* (34) considers that Catholics must willingly acknowledge (*agnosco*) and esteem the truly Christian endowments which derive from our common heritage [...]. It is right and salutary to recognise (*agnosco*) the riches of Christ and the virtuous deeds in the lives of others. While the Catholic Church does not recognise other churches as churches in the full sense of the term, it does recognise certain spiritual treasures in them.

In the Eastern Churches in particular, Christ can be "acknowledged (*agnosceretur*) as being truly and properly Son of God and son of man, according to the Scriptures". Catholics "must recognize (*agnoscendum est*) the admirable way in which they (the theological traditions of the Eastern Church) have their roots in holy scripture". Eastern theological language is considered "mutually complementary rather than conflicting" with Catholic statements (*Unitatis redintegratio*, 1617). In this sense, some horizontal recognition takes place between different ecclesiastical traditions. It can thus be argued that the Council develops a certain politics of multiculturalism and a recognition of otherness.

This vocabulary of Vatican II was further developed by Heinrich Fries, Walter Kasper and Joseph Ratzinger in their ecumenical writings during the 1970s. Kasper and Ratzinger emphasise that the recognition of other parties does not proceed in a diplomatic manner but it remains a spiritual and theological act which assumes a new orientation of the one who recognises. Heinrich Fries writes that, on the one hand, recognition of others expresses a legitimate theological plurality. On the other hand, a relationship of mutual recognition also assumes a common ground (*ein Gemeinsames*), which can bridge the differences.[41] This position of Fries resembles the ecumenical method of differentiating consensus, as employed in the Lutheran – Roman Catholic document *Joint Declaration on the Doctrine of Justification* (1999).[42]

In some sense, Vatican II and theological discussions deriving from it revive the old Christian way of speaking about *agnitio*, a recognition that also means metanoia and even conversion. When Ratzinger and Kasper emphasise that recognition is a spiritual act, they are also reviving the first and second paradigm in which recognition is far more than a change in its object's status. In the first and second paradigm, the change of the recognising subject remains within the focus of recognition. Therefore, theological recognition is different from political and diplomatic

---

[41] See Saarinen, *Recognition and Religion*, 176–180.
[42] For this method, see A. Birmelé/W. Thönissen (ed.), *Auf dem Weg zur Gemeinschaft* (Paderborn: Bonifatius, 2018).

processes of recognition. Conversion, or at least spiritual openness, is needed for the theological recognition of the other.

At the same time, such a spiritual emphasis does not mean subjectivism. Fries emphasises the importance of common ground with good reason. In addition to these Catholic considerations, I think that the third paradigm which emphasises the existential primacy of the subject does not aim at subjectivism as such. The modern Protestant paradigm, which leads from Spalding and Schleiermacher to Bultmann and Barth, wants to highlight the specific nature of theological acts of recognition.

In a modern world that separates religion from naturalism and science, theologians need to emphasise the importance of first-person stance and existential commitment. When we emphasise this, we do not aim at subjectivism but rather at an opening through which the intellectual resources of theology can be visible. This means *fides quaerens intellectum* rather than separatist fideism. Given this, the third paradigm, the existential status change in the object, is not very far from Kasper's and Ratzinger's ideas of spiritual recognition and interpersonal encounter.

In short, theologians already discussed the issues of recognition in depth in the 1970s. In social theory, we find similar discussions during the 1990s. Theologians were, for once, ahead of their times. The ecumenical documents which emerged from this trend often employ explicitly the language of mutual acknowledgement and recognition. They do not compare ecumenical recognition with political or diplomatic acts but affirm the specific theological nature of ecumenical encounter.

A good example of this kind is the so-called Porvoo Declaration, a full communion agreement between the Church of England and the Northern European Lutheran Churches. This document repeatedly uses the formula "we acknowledge" to lay out the mutual understanding reached in matters of faith. While the agreement assumes equality and lasting difference between the partner Churches, it also declares their readiness to be open to changes.[43] Although the drafters of the Porvoo Declaration may not have been aware of the long history of theological recognition, they have practised and continued it in their ecumenical formulations. I hope that the increasing awareness of the history of theological recognition paradigms may assist contemporary Christians and their churches in encountering other churches and other religions in terms of genuine equality and sincere difference.

---

[43] See Saarinen, *Recognition and Religion*, 180–182.

Methodological Principles: Luther, the Representative of a "World We Have Lost"
Heinz Schilling

The *histoire intellectuelle* of the Reformer has to be written with a, so to speak, anthropological approach, that is to say, with an awareness of the distance between the world of Luther and our own and of the fundamental differences not only in institutions and structures but, even more significantly, in beliefs, thought, behaviour, values and the basic principles of culture, politics and society. The person and character of Luther, his thinking and acting, can be rendered comprehensible only by referring to his self-understanding as God's prophet and his corresponding interpretation of his age as a moment of an eschatological battle between God and the devil, both taken to be real actors on earth – ideas and categories that are totally lacking in the modern mind and western civilisation.

Luther's distance from the modern world applies to nearly all the fundamental principles of western societies: his understanding of 'freedom', developed in his famous pamphlet of 1520 *Von der Freiheit eines Christenmenschen* (*A Treatise on Christian Liberty*), does not correspond to liberalism with its meaning of political and social liberty.[1] He did not favour tolerance – on the contrary, this was a totally alien category to him, as he was convinced that only religious unity could guarantee the peaceful conviviality of the community, territory or city, something basic to his attitudes towards the Jews. His ideas of politics and society were shaped by the early modern authoritarian state (*Obrigkeitsstaat*), not by models of political participation, not to mention democracy. The same is true of his standards in the relationship between males and females and their interaction in marriage, the family and the household. His economic principles stood in opposition to the early capitalism of the large, southern German commercial companies, and his subsequent focus on the question of *Wucher* (usury) weighed heavily in his relationships with Jews. Finally, and most importantly, his idea of religion, characterised by the eschatological relation between the earthly and the transcendent world and by an absolute claim of exclusive truth for his own interpretation of the Holy Scripture, is not compatible with the understanding of religion in modern societies.

Consequently, the Reformer must not be judged by our cultural and intellectual standards, and, vice versa, it is not possible to draw from his teaching or actions direct

---

[1] Cf. the most recent, newly annotated edition by T. Kaufmann, *An den christlichen Adel deutscher Nation, von des christlichen Standes Besserung* (Tübingen: Mohrsiebeck, 2014), with many references to *Freiheit* in the subject index.

instructions for our actions in the present and future. Luther can no longer be for his followers the paragon he has been for nearly half a millennium, the paragon that he was especially in certain periods, such as the nineteenth and early-twentieth centuries, both in Germany and in the world in general.

The methodological principle needed in order to make Luther's thinking and behavior understandable, reflecting on the specific historical structure of his time, by no means signifies accepting or even confirming his arguments and excusing his deeds, let alone denying any problematic or negative consequences for the cultural, political or social tradition. The biographer has to cope with finding a balance between historical fairness and the analytical evaluation of the consequences: s/he has to make the feelings, thoughts and actions of the 'hero' comprehensible without being trapped by ideology. This is particularly obvious with regard to Luther's attitude towards the Jews.

1. *New Principles in Commemorating Luther and the Reformation*

During the nineteenth century, parallel to Germany's rise to an economic, intellectual and political world power, German Protestant memorial policy started to celebrate the Reformation as a landmark in world history and a decisive engine of modernity. The tone was set by the head of German Idealism, the Berlin philosopher Georg Wilhelm Friedrich Hegel. Hegel identified Luther and the

Reformation as the break-through of *Innerlichkeit und Individualität* (inwardness and individuality), which in his eyes were constitutive for the modern world – in contrast to the Middle Ages, when man could not act according to his or her inwardness and individuality but was subordinated to forces lying outside his or her personality. This assessment was substantiated by Max Weber and Georg Jellinek, making Protestantism achieve a monopoly in the rise of capitalism and democracy.

Nineteenth-century historians and philosophers, along with Hegel and Leopold von Ranke in particular, turned Luther into the hero of a new age, providing the Protestant bourgeoisie of Germany with a philosophical and historical rationale for deploying the Reformer in their response to the rapid advance of modernisation in their own age. The interpretation of the Wittenberger's actions as revolutionary served to legitimise their world-altering activities and to place Germany at the head of progress. That Protestant historical model proved so powerful that on the eve of the fall into National Socialist barbarity, Adolf von Harnack, the most significant Protestant theologian and director of scholarship in the early twentieth century, was able to pronounce without any qualms that "the modern age began along with Luther's Reformation on 31 October 1517; it was inaugurated by the blows of the hammer on the door of the castle church at Wittenberg".[2]

---

[2] A. von Harnack, *Erforschtes und Erlebtes* (Berlin: De Gruyter, 1923), 110.

In the meantime, the mandarins of the German academic world are gone, and with them their grand picture of a eurocentric world history, as well. The memorial culture, which shapes the fifth centennial of the Reformation, is quite different. It is characterised:
- a) by a democratic and pluralistic instead of a monarchist authoritarian atmosphere;
- b) by endeavouring for ecumenical understanding instead of hostility and zeal for confessional dissociation;
- c) by a global perspective instead of euro-centrism – although in public discussion both politicians and religious people like to claim Luther and the Reformation as one of the starting points of western values.

2. A Faith That Is of the World

Against his will, Luther witnessed the birth of the pluralistic and liberal modern age; indirectly and involuntarily, he contributed to the emergence of modern tolerance, pluralism and liberalism and to the economics of modern society. His deliberate, personal legacy to the modern age lies elsewhere, in the rediscovery of religion and faith as elemental forces for the individual and for society. Just when the lustre of religion threatened to be overcome by the aesthetic and political brilliance of the secularised Renaissance papacy, the Wittenberg monk defined humankind's relationship with God anew and restored to religion its existential plausibility. His bold reasoning and courageous presence provided religion with the position it would then hold for centuries to come, in both private and public life in the modern age. As a result of the Protestant Reformation and the reformation of the papal church, for which Luther had provided the impetus, religion influenced the culture, society and, last but not least, politics of the modern age and was therefore able to play a decisive role in the radical transition that produced the European modern age.

The rebellion of the Wittenberg Augustine monk, motivated by his concern about salvation, turned the sixteenth century into an era that would be eulogised by Johann Wolfgang Goethe as an epoch "in which faith ruled". Renaissance, humanism and, above all, the Roman Curia, with its worldly involvement in power politics and artistic statements, had been treating religion as a splendid ornamentation of culture and philosophy; an apprehensive people had either to be content with empty sacred routine or to take refuge in the irrational practices of popular religion. However, Luther gave religion a new legitimacy and a new reality by means of a radical new understanding of a personal God through whose grace all people are drawn into relationship with Him without any need for intermediaries or ritual. God again became real – in the souls of the people and in their daily activities in the world. For many people, both educated and uneducated, both lords and subjects, both rich and poor, religion had been given back its existential significance and became the guiding principle for all thoughts and actions. The search for a single defining quality acquired by history from Luther and the Reformation, for what was singular and exceptional, leads us to this qualitative renewal of religion. That innovation had its roots in the theology and devotional practices of the late Middle Ages but it flowered only with Luther.

More important still is that Luther redirected the secularisation that had taken hold of religion into a new 'worldliness' (*Welthaftigkeit*). Previously monasteries, abbeys, religious foundations and other consecrated sites had provided the principal, and prominent, setting for faith and for the activities that sprang from it; now the Christian individual and Christendom as a whole were to live out their faith and prove themselves in their faith in their everyday experiences in the world.

Luther's teaching on justification, which formed the theological core of his rebellion against the papal church, reached out beyond the narrowly religious to have momentous impact on mentalities and behaviour. The transition from medieval works-based piety to evangelical grace-based devotion founded on the by faith alone principle set a course towards a modern vocational ethic that determined the Christian's correct activity in the world. The 'holiness' previously reserved for the priestly life, and especially for the life of the monk, was now brought out into the world. In serving the community (*ecclesia*), the family (*oeconomia*) and the state (*politia*), this holiness provided a new dynamic that had previously been held back from the world by the special status of the clerical calling (*vocatio*).

With Luther's eschatological theology uniting faith and world and identifying the world as the place where salvation unfolded, that which was of the world became part of salvation. Marriage, sexuality, work, and politics were all re-evaluated and given a new legitimacy. A dynamic that had been absent when medieval performance-based devotion had held sway was now present in both private and public life. To believe without acting in the world was now just as sinful and far from God as was acting in the world without believing. On this basis religion would help shape the modern world for centuries, culturally, socially, and politically.

Our image of the emergence of the modern age in Europe is distorted if on one hand we stamp Luther a revolutionary because he took on the authorities of his own time and yet on the other hand deem his focus on religion and the resultant confessional era a step backwards, a form of demodernisation, leading away from the rationalism and freedom of the Renaissance. Instead, we need to recognise that in assigning religion an original authority, subservient to neither philosophy nor art, and in identifying the world as the setting in which religion functioned and proved itself, Luther unleashed a dynamic that contributed fundamentally to the secular reshaping of early modern Europe and, in the longer term, to the emergence of the modern.

3. *State and Politics*

In the secular world, the impetus Luther brought to the processes of differentiation above all benefitted the early modern state, first in the Protestant parts of Europe and then, in modified form, in Catholic lands. Soon after Luther's death, the authorities in the evangelical territories of Germany seized the opportunity to bring the recently created territorial churches directly under their jurisdiction. They claimed decision-making power not only for the external affairs of their territorial churches but also, on occasion, for internal matters such as ritual and confession, an authority that Luther had unwaveringly reserved for theologians. In addition, they claimed extensive competence in matters previously solely, or largely, in the hands of the church and, in so doing, gained access to core activities of the modern state, such as care for the sick, old and needy, the regulation and control of marriage and the family, schooling and university education. The issues in which the state could intervene were now far more numerous. At the same time, political affairs continued to become more autonomous or secularised, so that politicians gradually felt released from the religious-based responsibilities that in his teaching on the two kingdoms Luther had imposed on Christian authorities in the world.

This territorial church governance of later Lutheranism saw religion not infrequently as a tool that could be employed to political or social ends, a development that was not in accord with Luther's fundamental principle of the freedom and right to self-determination of the church, both as a community and for the individual Christian. The Saxon Reformer would have had no time for the ideology of 'Throne and Altar' dominant in nineteenth-century Prussia and, incidentally, a product in many ways of traditional Hohenzollern 'court Calvinism'. The alliance with the National Socialists entered into by individual Lutheran bishops and German Christians could in no way be reconciled with his teachings. Yet these developments, the grim result of Luther's decision to commission the princes as emergency bishops for the cause of the Gospel, are also part of the history of Luther's influence.

The outcome was similar when it came to political activity and political consciousness more generally. Luther did not believe himself to be at the beck and call of the secular authorities. For the sake of peace and good order he demanded obedience to lawful authorities; a servile spirit and obedience for obedience's sake were, however, entirely alien to him. If pure teaching and the evangelical ordering of state and society were in danger, then dissent and Christian self-assertion, and any concomitant suffering, were required. He acknowledged an active right of resistance for individuals and authorities, who were thus constitutionally empowered. Despite the acceptance of an extensive role for the state in ecclesiastical affairs from the mid-sixteenth century, the memory of Luther's successful rebellion against traditional authority remained alive in Lutheran churches and could be deployed to justify both individual and collective actions. The lay Christian participated in the life of the church in concrete form every Sunday, not simply passively, in hearing the word of God, but also actively, in confessing the evangelical faith and, above all, in singing hymns. The independence of the pastors was not completely eradicated with their submission to the supervisory authority of the temporal authorities: on the whole, the Lutheran pastorates behaved like loyal employees of the state, but some pastors and theologians were prepared to drag princes and magistrates over the coals as Luther himself had always done. Greater engagement with authorities brought with it a more deeply rooted willingness, even responsibility, to censure those same authorities. Even though the right of active resistance was limited to specific office holders, on occasion Lutheran Christians were both ready and able to resist actively in response to injustice.

And yet, the early modern urban, territorial, or – as in Sweden – national churches eclipsed the freedom of the self-determining Christian and the early communal church. While civic Calvinism remained firmly anchored in the political culture of western Europe, the tradition of a civic Lutheranism in central and northern Europe, which in the mid-sixteenth century had still been capable of collective political action, even active resistance, faded away. The two branches of the Reformation, therefore, contributed in different ways to the creation of an open, participatory political culture, partly as a result of their singular origins. Calvinism drew on a tradition of underground, exiled or independent churches free of secular authority and on the maritime and libertarian character of western Europe, in particular in the Dutch mercantile Republic. Other than in a few solitary communities, neither feature shaped German Lutheranism.

The broader historical context sent the church in a specific direction, but so, too, did Luther. He never disavowed the rudiments of the communal church found in his early theology but he subsequently embedded them within the structures of the territorial church. While, as we have seen, that tactic was based on an accurate assessment of prevailing power constellations, it decisively weakened the communal principle. The sense of political responsibility that was both deep-rooted and pervasive in Calvinist societies did not develop under Lutheran auspices. Democratic tendencies associated with the self-government of church and community have correctly been linked to the presbyterial and synodial constitution of Calvinism, but any such democratic leanings were impeded in Lutheranism. The transition to the modern form of participatory evangelical lay church took place for Lutheranism only in the nineteenth century, and even then it faced resistance. Luther and his reception played their part in ensuring that in nineteenth-century Germany, a "delayed nation", had to begin its "long road West".[3]

4. *Christians and Jews*

The biographer has to make the thoughts, feelings and actions of his 'hero' understandable without being trapped in his own ideology. This is especially obvious with regard to Luther's attitude towards the Jews.

---

[3] For "delayed nation", cf. H. Plessner, *Die verspätete Nation* (Stuttgart: W. Kohlhammer, 1959); for "long road West", H.A. Winkler, *Der lange Weg nach Westen* (7th edn; 2 vol.; Munich: C.H. Beck, 2010); English translation, *Germany: The Long Road West*, trans. A.J. Sager, (2 vol.; Oxford: Oxford University Press, 2000).

4.1 The Historical Facts

The Reformer was on several occasions concerned with Jews, their religion, their meaning for Christian theology and their position within Christian society. The first pamphlet was extremely friendly and positive, which was quite exceptional in the Christian tradition and allegedly marked a turning point in Christian-Jewish relations. In contrast, the later pamphlets were radically negative and of a rhetoric that indeed is close to the hate campaigns of the Nazis. Indeed, Julius Streicher, chief ideologist and editor of *Der Stürmer*, actually tried to exculpate himself at the Nurnberg trial by arguing that Martin Luther himself should have been sitting in the dock next to him.

How can we explain Luther's radical change from being a friend and defender to a merciless pursuer of the Jews? Luther was brought up and lived for a lifetime in a region where for decades Jews were not allowed to settle and obtained only exceptional concessions to travel or do business. Consequently, Luther had little or no contact with Jewish people. Jews were not the object of his thoughts concerning the political, social or economic dimension of daily life but exclusively of his theology, although in the end this had far-reaching consequences for the form of daily life within the new evangelical cities and territories. The first pamphlet *Daß Jesus Christus ein geborener Jude sei* was published in 1523 on the apogee of the Reformation process in Germany, when Luther hoped, indeed he was sure, that the "new light of the evangelical truth" would soon be accepted not only within the Christian church as a whole but also by Jews.

In his eyes, the only reason why the Jews had not already become Christians was the papal torsion of Christ's teaching. Now, as the original version of the evangelical truth was reestablished by his Reformation theology, the truth of Christ's word had become evident to everybody. Consequently, all people of goodwill should convert to Christendom, in the first place the Jews, the brethren of the Saviour.

The attacks on the Jews started in the late 1530s, when Luther definitively realised that his early hopes for their conversion had not been effected. He felt deeply disappointed and consequently his sentiment turned to a radical anti-Judaism, and it became full of hate during the last decade of his life, when he was painfully afflicted by chronic as well as acute diseases and when he – even more importantly – suffered from the anxiety that after his imminent death his Reformation would be destroyed by the military actions of the Emperor and his Catholic allies. He was driven by a kind of pathologic psychosis that after his death Jews would present a fundamental danger to the newly established purity of evangelical communities. In his eyes, the Jews were agents of the devil, who was eager to extinguish once again the light of evangelical truth revealed to Christianity by the Reformation. This was the political and psychological background to Luther's later, dreadful *Judenschriften*, which today, after the holocaust experience of the twentieth century, are necessarily an indescribable scandal. In 1543, Luther published in rapid sequence (January, March and July) three pamphlets *Von den Juden und ihren Lügen, Von Schem Hamphoras und vom Geschlecht Christi, Von den Letzten Worten Davids.*[4] In these publications, replete with hateful attacks and insults, he reproduces all the anti-Judaic clichés of the medieval Christian mentality, which in 1523 in his first, positive *Judenschrift* he had declared as *Märlein*, erroneous stories of the papal church. His arguments end with the advice to the territorial princes and urban magistrates to burn the synagogues and Jewish schools, take their books away, outlaw any teaching on the part of the rabbis and all economic activities, apart from working on the land by hand with the most simple instruments.

When Luther, already old and severely ill, caught a cold on his last trip to Mansfeld in early 1546, he blamed the tiny Jewish settlement that he had passed through, one of the very rare ones still existing in this region. Travelling through their streets he had felt an icy wind blowing into his open wagon – without doubt a magic attack on his health, carried out by the agents of the devil, who with his death wanted to destroy the Reformation settlement. During the following stay in the Earldom of Mansfeld, although he was deeply engaged in very complicated negotiations for settling a conflict between the different branches of the dynasty, he preached nearly every day in the city church of St Andreas. On Monday, February 15, he concluded his sermon by reading from the pulpit the *Vermahnung wider die Juden* (*Admonition to the magistrates, here concretely the Earls of Mansfeld, against the Jews*). As his

---

[4] Luther, WA 53, 417–552, 573–648; Luther, WA 54, 28–100.

health condition declined dramatically the next day and he died overnight between Wednesday and Thursday, the *Vermahnung* became his last public statement and consequently a kind of last will. Although the rhetoric is not as aggressive and hateful as in the pamphlets mentioned above, especially *Of the Jews and their lies*, his advice is clear and straightforward: there is no longer any hope that the Jews will be ready for baptism. On the contrary, they are daily ridiculing and making derisive remarks about Christ and his mother Mary. Consequently, anybody who tolerates this situation is guilty before God – even more the magistrates since they are responsible for the salvation, or non-salvation, of their subjects. The only remedy is for all princes and city magistrates to expel the Jews immediately from their territories in order to make Christian society pure and eliminate any un-Christian temptation or moral or dogmatic conflict.

Almost none of the German princes or city magistrates was ready to follow this advice. Nevertheless, Luther's pamphlets against the Jews were part of Lutheran identity, although for a long time kept somewhat in the background and even criticised, especially by pietistic theologians.[5] When, during the second half of the nineteenth century, the early modern anti-Judaism was transformed

---

[5] J. Wallmann, "The Reception of Luther's Writings on the Jews from the Reformation to the End of the 19th Century", in *Lutheran Quarterly* 1 (1987) 72–97; J. Wallmann, *Pietismusstudien, Gesammelte Aufsätze* (Tübingen: Mohr Siebeck, 2008).

into the ethnic anti-Semitism of modern times,[6] fierce anti-Semites within the Protestant Church, for example. Adolf Stoecker, Prussian *Hof- und Domprediger* at Berlin, could and did use Luther as a reference, although the Reformer himself adhered to the religious argument, even in his last days:

> *Wo sie sich aber bekeren, ihren Wucher sein lassen Christum annehmen, so wollen wir sie gerne, als unsere Brüder halten. Anders wird nichts draus/* If they are ready for conversion and stop with usury and accept Christ, then we are happy to regard them as our brethren. Otherwise it will not work.[7]

The racist Nazi propagandists even blamed the Lutheran church for hiding Luther's racism and claimed to be his real interpreters and true heirs.[8]

Our second argument makes a plea for a shift in the discussion of the topic 'Jews and Protestants' (and Christians in general): a shift from *anti* to *con*, from anti-Semitism to Christian-Jewish interaction focusing on eclipsing processes and developments in either (or both?) culture.

---

[6] H. Berding, *Moderner Antsemitismus in Deutschland* (Frankfurt a. M.: Suhrkamp, 1988).
[7] WA 51, 195.
[8] T. Kaufmann, *Luthers Juden* (Ditzingen: Reclam, 2014), 160ff. The reception of Luther's *Judenschriften* during the nineteenth and twentieth centuries was discussed at Erlangen University in the autumn of 2014. The contributions will be published by Anselm Schubert.

4.2 Long Term Impact

Evaluating Luther's long-term impact on the relationship between Christians and Jews is particularly challenging: Luther's religiously and eschatologically founded anti-Judaism is not the same as modern racial anti-Semitism. His call on the German authorities to expel the Jews, like in Spain and England, was not designed to lead to their extermination and was not a precursor of the Holocaust carried out under National Socialism. No direct path led from Luther to Hitler. However, the Reformation cannot be acquitted of the charge that its unbounded attacks (albeit not on those who were ethnically other, only on religious outsiders and those who 'denied the truth') helped poison attitudes towards Jews in the nineteenth and twentieth centuries. Luther's later Jewish writings would not have been read in every Protestant household, not even in the homes of all the pastors, but his attitude towards Jews was well known and would have had an impact simply because Luther was Luther, and in the nineteenth century Luther was re-imagined by his supporters as a superhuman hero of the German people.

Individual Lutheran Christians, just like individual Catholics, Calvinists and Anglicans, took a courageous stand against the racial fanaticism of the National Socialists and aided threatened Jews, but the Lutheran confessional culture failed to erect a firewall against the National Socialist destructive mania. In countries in western Europe, where Reformed Protestantism was very influential, an intellectual exchange between Jews and Christians had begun in the seventeenth century, and for residents of towns such as Amsterdam the coexistence of Christians and Jews was taken for granted. That reality was to some extent a product of the distinct social and economic situation in western Europe, but it also stemmed from the ecclesiastical and theological tradition, and then again from the experience of the diaspora and otherness that generations of Calvinists shared with Jews, not infrequently even in one and the same location, such as in Hamburg.

A number of Lutheran communities also endured flight, expulsion, and minority status, and in the Catholic Rhineland were even persecuted, living 'under the cross', like members of underground churches. Yet theirs was not the widely disseminated, collective experience that might have moulded Lutheran confessional culture and sown seeds of sympathy for the other or for minorities. From the outset, Luther had been incapable of dialogue with those who did not think as he did, the downside to the prophetic self-confidence that was essential for his success. Furthermore, he never suffered anything like the personal experience of exile of Reformed theologians, such as John Calvin or John à Lasco – the latter left Poland for Emden and London, from where he was expelled; then, in the harshness of winter, with his foreign community he was denied refuge in the ports of Denmark and northern Germany. In his final years, as we have seen, believing the final eschatological battle was at hand, Luther developed what was well-nigh a phobia about all that was alien. His norm was and remained the single-faith pure society in which ecclesiastical and civic communities were indistinguishable.

5. *Freedom of Conscience and Its Pre-Modern Meaning*

With the abolition of the priestly estate, whose sanctified members were able to intervene before God, every Protestant Christian now had a direct relationship with God. They no longer had to be prepared to defend their thoughts and actions before the hierarchy of the church for they were now responsible only to their consciences. Although it was revolutionary in the context of the age of the Reformation, this new understanding did not usher in individualism and subjectivism in the modern sense. To find early signs of it we must look instead to the aesthetic and philosophical thinking of the Renaissance, to Albrecht Dürer's individualistic artistic approach, for example, or to Ulrich von Hutten's authorial subjectivity. For Luther, Christian identity, characterised by a direct, personal connection to God, was realised within a community, as were Christian freedom and the priesthood of all believers; the upshot was the development of new spheres of action, but not as a precursor of liberalism or a plurality of opinion. For Luther, freedom came with "bondage" (*Knechtschaft*) in the form of ties to Christian norms, in particular in a commitment to the wellbeing of one's neighbour.

For Luther, moreover, freedom of conscience, which he had advocated so strongly in Worms, meant in concrete terms imprisonment in the word of God, being bound by religion. He understood 'conscience' as a theological quality that was associated not with behaviour but with the person, with the being and the salvation of the individual. A good conscience is not a sign of conformity with norms and moral codes; a good conscience is, simply, faith.

The Lutheran idea of the priesthood of all believers posited that all people are fundamentally equal before God, in particular in the light of God's assurance of salvation. When it came to ecclesiastical reality, however, Luther juxtaposed the priesthood of all believers with the office of pastor. In Lutheranism, the priesthood of the faithful was supplemented – or, we might say, mitigated – by the preacher and pastor, who alone were permitted to proclaim the word and administer the sacraments, having been expressly approved for these roles by their training, call and ordination. This pastoral preaching was performed within a church, set apart as a consecrated building. Within Lutheranism the church building became, and remained, a sacred site for the worship of God and proclamation of God's word.

> On this point Luther had retreated for in 1520, in his 'Treatise on Good Works', which admonished the pope for the ostentation of his church buildings, Luther had explained that prayer 'under a straw roof or in a pigsty' was far more threatening to the papacy than magnificent churches that lacked such 'unconquerable prayer'. He backed down from that position soon after, alarmed by the protests of the 'false brothers' against all external order, holding that preaching should be held in 'an orderly, public, reverent assembly ... and one should not seek out secret concerns to hide away, as the Anabaptists do'.[9]

---

[9] H. Schilling, *Martin Luther, Rebell in Einer Zeit des Umbruchs. Eine Biographie* (3rd edn; Munich: C.H. Beck, 2014), 633.

Politically and socially, too, no room was left for freedom of conscience in its modern sense. For Luther, Europe and Christendom were identical. At best, Jews or even Muslims could live here only with special permission, and that authorisation could be revoked. It was the duty of the authorities to ensure that every individual was baptised immediately after birth and thereby admitted into the Christian community and the church. Rejection of infant baptism or the Trinity was a punishable act, in no way different from atheism.

6. *The Impact on Catholicism*

As the Wittenberg Reformation stood its ground against all that Rome and the Emperor could throw at it and with the creation of additional Protestant churches elsewhere – Reformed and Calvinist in Switzerland and western Europe, Anglican in England – Europe experienced a powerful shift towards ideological and institutional diversity. The early modern confessional churches with their confessional cultures made a profound impression on the continent, in the intellectual and cultural, and well as political and social, fields. That impact was a product of mutual antagonism, even enmity, but it also resulted from fruitful competition in response to provocation, and not infrequently, was generated by osmosis and exchange.

Luther was successful even, and specifically, in Rome. Medieval traditions fostered the papal church's early modern revival, but in the face of opposition from a more powerful curia, the reforming enthusiasm of the late medieval period had largely tailed off by the beginning of the sixteenth century. Rome needed to hear the wakeup call that rang out from Wittenberg if it was to launch the rapid renewal necessary to ensure that it was not left at a considerable disadvantage. In the end, the Roman reforms also permitted a transition into the modern age, even if that process was built on spiritual and institutional foundations that were not those of the societies and churches of the Reformation.[10]

The papal church that emerged from the reforming Council of Trent was not the medieval, universal church against which Luther had rebelled. Just like the confessional churches of the Reformation, the Tridentine Catholic confessional church was also a new church of a modern age. After Luther, the popes were even more reliant on the assistance of the secular rulers than they had been when under threat from late medieval conciliarism. As a result, even in Catholic areas of Germany and Europe, the religious and ecclesiastical authority that had been exercised by the church now passed into the hands of the state. Much as in Protestant areas, that process was connected to the territorialisation and regionalisation of organisations and administration, in Catholic lands above all when it came to the appointment of bishops and the authority

---

[10] This verdict, which diverges from the position taken in older work on ecclesiastical history and the sociology of religion, is a product of the confessionalisation paradigm.

over the clergy in general. The Gallicanism of the modern age in France is merely the best-known example, for in the Spanish church and in the territories of the Empire that remained Catholic, above all the dukedom of Bavaria, the stronghold of the old faith in southern Germany, secular rulers dedicated a great deal of energy to ensuring that they also had a decisive say in the appointment of bishops, the administration and use of church property, the disciplinary supervision of the clergy, educational and training institutions, universities and colleges alike, ecclesiastical institutions that catered for social welfare or cared for the sick, and so on.

This Catholic renewal had Luther and his competing Protestant Reformation to thank above all for new impetuses in education. No less a figure than Jesuit Peter Canisius, so influential in southern Germany, soberly recorded that the Catholic Church had fallen behind when it came to schools and universities and he immediately launched himself into a race to catch up: in the Catholic areas of Germany his Counter-Reformation catechism performed a role very similar to that of the Lutheran catechism in Protestant territories.

Emulation of Luther's work on the catechism was only one element of Rome's extensive response. As in Protestant lands, new modes of thinking and behaving reached many layers of society, but in the early modern Tridentine church those innovations were the work of the reform orders, above all of the extensive Jesuit network, and were adopted in particular by princes and the nobility, by the new political and educational elites and by the burgher class. The rural areas were initially little affected, but the situation for Protestantism was hardly very different. In response to Luther, Catholic agents of confessionalisation also sought to effect the Christianisation of society as a whole, to encourage self-searching and self-direction, and to create a programmatic bond between religious interiority and a moral and responsible life within the family, the church and the town or village community. As a result of Luther's evangelical renewal, a modern Christianity also emerged within renewed Catholicism, fostering a bourgeois spirit (*esprit bourgeois*) throughout Europe. The efforts of the reform orders "contained enough novelty with regard to the family and society, as well as in the manner of living one's religion, to disquiet the champions of tradition", Louis Châtellier noted.[11] Where married and family life in the Luther house in Wittenberg served as the model for the Protestant burgher family, the cult of the Holy Family, promoted above all by the Jesuits, became exemplary in Catholic societies.

Without the pressure and challenge from Luther, the Renaissance papacy, characterised by Alexander VI Borgia, Julius II de la Rovere or even Leo X Medici, would hardly have been in a position to undertake such a radical revitalisation of religion. With the reforms of the Council of Trent, wrung from the popes only by Luther's

---

[11] L. Châtellier, *The Europe of the Devout: The Catholic Reformation and the Formation of a New Society* (Cambridge: Cambridge University Press, 1987), 135, III.

European-wide success, religion re-emerged as the focus of the papal church, enabling it to make its own contribution to the history of the modern age in Europe. The successful staging of religion celebrated by today's popes, among young people in particular, is also a sign of Luther's success, for the reformer remedied religion's developing anaemia and reinstated its existential power. The Catholic Church may not want to celebrate the five-hundredth anniversary in 2017, but it should feel invited to join with the Lutherans in honouring the Reformation.

7. The End of Universalism and the Rise of Modern Differentiation in European Religion and Culture

Like all the other leading figures of his age, Luther understood religion in universal terms, since, for the reformer, it was the sole truth for an evangelically renewed Christendom. As God's prophet, he was responsible for bringing that truth, which alone could save, to all peoples and for ensuring its implementation everywhere. Charles V's universal political project failed, but so too did Luther's universal theological and ecclesiastical plan. The outcome was momentous. Cultural and political differentiation within Europe, the modern concept of liberty, and in the long term even the ideological pluralism without which modern society would be unthinkable, were all only possible when universalism no longer held sway. Such ideas would have been utterly alien to both Emperor and Reformer.

The Habsburgs could not prevail against the militant particularism of separatist territories and nations. Kings, princes and their subjects were no longer prepared to form a single universal *populus Christianus*, with the emperor as *sacerdos Christi*, Christ's anointed one, their representative and ruler. The future belonged to 'sovereignty', the aspiration of all rulers and republican magistrates, with its theoretical foundations supplied by French royal jurist Jean Bodin.

Nevertheless, the emperor was able to safeguard the authority of the Habsburg family, although he did so not through a universal monarchy but by means of a dual hegemony established at the time of his abdication, when his authority was divided:

– between the Spanish Habsburg line, which retained its supremacy for another century;

– and the Austrian Habsburg line, which exercised Habsburg interests in central and eastern Europe for nearly another 400 years.

The real loser in the creation of this new political and cultural order in Europe was the pope. The Roman Church retained its claims to universality, even though that universality had become a fiction after the self-assertion of the Reformation; the papal church was now a modern particularistic confessional church just like its Reformation rivals.

Despite the splendid symbolical representation of the papacy's claims to universality by the splendid reorganisation of the Eternal City by Sixtus V, at the end of the Reformation century, and the universalistic gesture of the design of Saint Peter's Square by Gian Lorenzo Bernini half a century later, the particularity and political insignificance of the papacy were in practice very evident: at the peace conference held at Münster at the end of the Thirty Years War, the cause of which had been the struggle for religious and territorial power, the curia fought tooth and nail against the secular political order of the Peace of Westphalia, but the international community of states, both Catholic and Protestant alike, simply brushed aside its protests.

Protestantism, on the other hand, became an engine of differentiation, though in no way intended to be such by Luther and his co-Reformers: Luther's original concept of a universal reformation of the church and the world failed, but its very failure launched fundamental cultural and social-political change in Europe, and later in other parts of the world, too. Abandoned by the universal authorities of church and Empire, Luther entered instead into an alliance with the princes and the early modern state, and in the process became the Reformer, and finally even church father, of a new evangelical faith and of a modern particularistic confessional church. Without questioning the universality of faith and of the invisible church, Luther demolished medieval universalism and repudiated the legitimacy of its dual imperial-papal leadership. Ecclesiastical and confessional differentiation lent further impetus to the political and social differentiation in Christendom that had begun in the late medieval period, driving it onwards to the birth, in the firestorm of the European confessional wars, of an international system comprising legally equal, particular states.

Methodological Principles

Undoubtedly, this cultural, political and ideological differentiation within Europe had its roots in the Middle Ages, but it was Luther and the Reformation that gave it its religious legitimacy and modern dynamic. In the long term, this process fostered the shift to the secularism, pluralism and freedom of conscience of the modern age. That had not been Luther's goal, either, but was another unintended consequence of his thinking and his acting.

As a consequence of the Reformation – not so much of its theology, but of the simple fact that it was able to survive – the uniform (integrated) nucleus of European civilisation, the Christian religion, broke up. This was the precondition for the opening of Europe's door to cultural and societal differentiation, first to a multi-confessional Christianity, and later to a pluralistic religious and ideological civilisation. Consequently, Europe's modern identity is characterised by both a sense of difference and by one of unity at the same time.

Nearly 500 years after Luther's Reformation Giorgio Strehler, one of the leading European intellectuals and famous director of Milan's Piccolo Teatro, put it like this: Europe's cultural identity means "never to think of one country or one culture in any other way than with regard to other countries and cultures".

At the time of the five-hundredth anniversary of Luther's 95 theses, the different Christian churches have become accustomed to thinking of, and defining, themselves without hostility, that is to say, not as contrary but in relation to each other. The same is true with regard to Christian and Jewish relationships – and will, or must, also be true in the future with regard to Islam and all other religions, as well as to the rising number of non-believers.

However, one of the most important consequences of the European experiences of the Reformation and its political, social and cultural effects, the peaceful conviviality of different churches or religions, will not function by declaring religious truth as irrelevant. The different religions, as well as the non-believers, must be integrated into peaceful secular civil society, which means that they have to learn to bear, and cope with, the differences of the respective religious or ideological truths, in the best case to take pleasure in the differences and variety of spirituality and rites.

A Fractal Interpretation of Religious Diversity

Perry Schmidt-Leukel

In this paper I would like to introduce a new interpretation of religious diversity. I call it a 'fractal interpretation' because the theory claims that religious diversity displays a fractal structure. Actually, like so many 'new' theories, this fractal interpretation is not entirely new. It has been, as I shall explain shortly, anticipated in the phenomenology of religions, in inter-cultural philosophy and even, to some extent, in the religions themselves. As far as my own intellectual development is concerned, I now realise that I was 'pregnant' with this theory for something like three decades – an unusually long pregnancy, I have to admit. It was only in 2015, when I was preparing my Gifford Lectures,[1] that the theory was born. In the middle of the night, at about 3 am, labor set in. I woke up, went to my desk and sketched on one or two sheets of paper how religious diversity can be best understood along the lines of fractal structures.

---

[1] The present paper contains some material from P. Schmidt-Leukel, *Religious Pluralism and Interreligious Theology. The Gifford Lectures – An Extended Edition* (Maryknoll, N.Y.: Orbis, 2017), 222-245.

My paper has four parts. First, I shall briefly explain the concept and nature of fractals and show how fractal structures are found in inorganic and organic nature. Second, I will move on to the realm of culture and religion. After discussing some precursors of a fractal interpretation of religious diversity, I shall quote, in the third part, some examples of how this theory is already at work in contemporary interreligious theology. In the fourth and final part, I shall briefly point out what I regard to be the advantages and fruitfulness of this theory.

1. *Fractals in Inorganic and Organic Nature*

In 1975, the mathematician Benoît Mandelbrot introduced the term 'fractal'. With fractals Mandelbrot was referring to certain patterns, structures or forms which display a rough or strict self-similarity across various scales, that is to say, a component of the pattern or structure constitutes either a strictly identical or at least a similar copy of the whole. Recursiveness and scale invariance are the two key elements of fractals. A well-known example of a fractal shape with strict self-similarity and scale invariance is the so-called Sierpinski triangle (fig. 1).

The triangle is composed of three smaller triangles which contain within themselves the same structure and composition of still smaller triangles, and so on.

Mandelbrot proposed that fractal structures with less strict and more irregular forms of self-similarity are found in a number of inorganic and organic natural

Figure 1. Sierpinski triangle.

phenomena.[2] He chose the term fractal because it was particularly well suited to describing these irregular forms of self-replication as they are often found in nature:

> I coined *fractal* from the Latin adjective *fractus*. The corresponding Latin verb *frangere* means 'to break': to create

[2] B.B. Mandelbrot, *The Fractal Geometry of Nature. Updated and augmented* (New York: W.H. Freeman, 1983), 1.

irregular fragments. It is therefore sensible – and how appropriate for our needs! – that, in addition to 'fragmented' (as in *fraction* or *refraction*), *fractus* should also mean 'irregular', both meanings being preserved in *fragment*.[3]

A prominent example of such non-strict self-similarity, or self-similarity in irregularity, are coast-lines. If one zooms into a coast-line, getting ever larger magnifications of ever smaller sections, one will notice self-similarity in the sense that one gets similarly fringed lines, with similar shapes like bays, fiords, spits or tongues, etcetera. Other well-known examples from inorganic nature are certain rock-formations or ice-crystals, each composed of smaller sections with similar, though irregular, structures. As a final example let me mention the structure of waves as it is so masterfully expressed in Hokusai's *The Great Wave* (fig. 2).[4]

A well-known organic example is a cauliflower, which is composed of various smaller florets, each of which resembles in its structure the cauliflower as a whole. A particularly beautiful variant of this is Romanesco, a near relative of cauliflower. The same fractal structure is also found in many trees (fig. 3) or fern leaves (fig. 4).

Given the pervasiveness of fractal phenomena, Mandelbrot emphasised "that the fractal approach is both effective and 'natural.' Not only should it not be resisted, but

---

[3] Ibid., 4.
[4] Source of the figure: http://www.delimited.io/blog/2014/2/24/fractals-in-d3-dragon-curves, 17 July 2018.

A Fractal Interpretation of Religious Diversity

Figure 2. Fractal structure of waves in Katsushika Hokusai's *The Great Wave*.

Figure 3. Fractal structure of trees.

Perry Schmidt-Leukel

Figure 4. Fractal structure of fern leaves.

Figure 5. Śrī Yantra or Śrī Chakra.

one ought to wonder how one could have gone so long without it".[5] His theory finally culminates in the thesis: "There is a fractal face to the geometry of nature".[6]

It seems that religions have at times had some awareness of the fractal structure of our world. I do not want to go into too much detail here, but rather I will proceed with just some brief examples.[7]

In Sufism there is the widespread saying: "The universe is a big man and man a little universe".[8] In other words, macrocosmic structures replicate on the microcosmic level, especially on the level of human existence. The conviction of a micro-macrocosmic parallelism is also widespread in Hinduism. That is, macrocosmic structures are replicated at the microcosmic level and vice versa. The idea of a fractal structure underlying the whole cosmos has been given a remarkable expression in the so-called Śrī *Yantra* or Śrī *Chakra* (fig. 5). The nine intersecting triangles are of a multilayered symbolic meaning. They circle around the fractal micro-macrocosm scheme, for example representing earth, air and sun as mirrored in body, breath and the inner light of consciousness paralleled

---

[5] Mandelbrot, *The Fractal Geometry of Nature*, 3.
[6] Ibid.
[7] For numerous examples of ideas in the world religions that come close to fractal concepts of reality see: W.J. Jackson, *Heaven's Fractal Net. Retrieving Lost Visions in the Humanities* (Bloomington: Indiana University Press, 2004), 28–59, 72–112.
[8] T. Burckhardt, *Introduction to Sufi Doctrine* (Bloomington: World Wisdom, 2008), 65.

with further sets of threes.⁹ The irregular, but nevertheless clearly fractal structure of the Śrī *Yantra* is evident.

Another, somewhat similar, example is the Buddhist idea of the world as Indra's Net which we find in the *Avataṃsaka* or *Kegon Sūtra*. Indra's Net consists of an infinite number of crystal pearls, all woven into a celestial net, such that the whole net of empty pearls is mirrored or replicated in each singe pearl.

My final example is taken from the *Bible moralisée*, a medieval picture Bible from the early thirteenth century (fig. 6).¹⁰ The frontispiece depicts the creation of the world in a way that is somewhat reminiscent of the micro-macrocosmos scheme. The image is often called *God as the architect of the world*. Yet this seems to be inaccurate. From the cross in the halo it is evident that the depicted 'architect' is not God the Father but Christ. This is in line with the ancient Christian and Platonic idea that God created the world through the Logos, that is, through the eternal word or mind of God, which later assumed human form in Jesus. This idea involves three interconnected levels: first, God as the ultimate source of everything, second, the Logos as the mind or word of God, and third, the world as created in and through the Logos. The image from the *Bible moralisée* shows this by giving the same colour to Christ's halo as to the orbit of the

---

⁹ See S. Kak, "The Great Goddess Lalitā and the Śrī Cakra", *Brahmavidyā: The Adyar Library Bulletin* 72–73 (2008–2009) 155–172.
¹⁰ Source of the figure: https://commons.wikimedia.org/wiki/File:God_the_Geometer.jpg, 17 July 2018.

A Fractal Interpretation of Religious Diversity

Figure 6. Anonymous, *God as Architect*, frontispiece of the Bible Moralisée, illumination on parchment, Wien, Austrian National Library, 1220-1230.

world. Another fractal touch is given by the fringes of the nocturnal sky, which exhibit a fractal pattern of the wave or coast-line type.

Let me now turn from inorganic and organic nature and move on to the realms of culture and religion, which also display a fractal face.

2. *Fractal Structures in Culture and Religion*

In 1975, Hajime Nakamura published his monumental intercultural and comparative history of ideas.[11] Nakamura concluded his voluminous study with the finding that, despite the differences between human cultures and traditions, in all of them "more or less the same problems arise".[12] This, says Nakamura, "means that human nature and human concerns are also vastly similar".[13] To a large extent, debates in contemporary inter-cultural philosophy oscillate between the two positions of a radical incommensurability of human cultures, on the one hand, and their complete commensurability or even essential identity, on the other, while trying to find a satisfactory middle path between these two extremes. As one such middle position, the Indian intercultural philosopher Ram Adhar Mall proposes

---

[11] H. Nakamura, *A Comparative History of Ideas* (London/New York: Kegan Paul, 1992).
[12] Ibid., 565.
[13] Ibid.

his concept of intercultural overlapping. Without any overlapping structures, intercultural understanding and communication would be impossible.[14] A similar position is taken by the German intercultural philosopher Bernhard Waldenfels. He goes one step further with his concept of intercultural intersection (*Verschränkung*), which means that what is culturally familiar and what is culturally alien "are more or less entangled with each other". The borderlines between cultures are fuzzy and are more about "accentuation, emphasis and statistic frequency than clear-cut differentiation".[15] Thus, in speaking of intercultural intersection, Waldenfels seeks to point out that one will find something of one's own culture in the foreign one and something of the foreign culture within one's own.[16] This is, *in nuce*, a fractal interpretation of cultural diversity, which Waldenfels finds substantiated by the work of the Swiss intercultural philosopher, Elmar Holenstein.

Holenstein, who taught at the Universities of Bochum, Zürich, Tokyo and Hong Kong, bases his observations primarily on his comparative studies of western and far eastern cultures. According to Holenstein, "it is possible to identify those structures, which are particularly strong in one culture, also (at least in rudimentary form) in (nearly

---

[14] R.A. Mall, *Intercultural Philosophy* (Lanham: Rowman & Littlefield Publishers, 2000), 13–24.
[15] Both quotations in B. Waldenfels, "Verschränkung von Heimwelt und Fremdwelt" in R.A. Mall/D. Lohmar (ed.), *Philosophische Grundlagen der Interkulturalität* (Amsterdam: Rodopi, 1995) 53–65, on p. 54 (my translation).
[16] Ibid., 56.

all) other cultures".[17] One of his examples is the rich variety of different degrees of politeness in the Japanese language. Idioms conveying various forms of politesse exist in all languages, but they are not everywhere as elaborate as in Japanese.[18] Assuming that one particular feature, or cluster of features, is exclusively present in just one culture while totally absent from another, would be misleading. Cultural differences, says Holenstein, are rather based on the cross-cultural distribution of various features, but with different hierarchies, emphases or different degrees of elaboration.[19] The variations between cultures are thus mirrored by the variations that we find within cultures or even within one individual person:[20]

> [...] the same oppositions that are thought to be ascertainable between two cultures (*interculturally*) can often be detected in the same kind and degree within one and the same culture (*intraculturally*), even within one and the same person (*intrasubjectively*) depending on age, surroundings, task or just on mood and humour.[21]

---

[17] E. Holenstein, *Menschliches Selbstverständnis. Ichbewußtsein – Intersubjektive Verantwortung – Interkulturelle Verständigung* (Frankfurt a. M.: Suhrkamp, 1985), 133 (my translation).
[18] Holenstein, *Menschliches Selbstverständnis*, 133.
[19] Ibid., 137ff.
[20] Ibid., 149ff.
[21] E. Holenstein, "A Dozen Rules of Thumb for Avoiding Intercultural Misunderstandings" *Polylog* 4 (2003) see: https://them.polylog.org/4/ahe-en.htm, 17 July 2018.

A Fractal Interpretation of Religious Diversity

In this important thesis, Holenstein distinguishes three different levels of diversity: the intercultural level, that is the global level of cultural diversity, the intracultural level, that is the diversity found within each culture, and the intrasubjective level, that is the diversity found within the mental cosmos of individual persons. What he actually says is that various patterns of cultural diversity replicate over these three levels or scales. The cultural diversity at the global level is reflected in the diversity within each culture and this again is, to some extent, reflected, on a still smaller scale, in individual persons. Holenstein therefore rejects the idea of a radical difference between cultures in favour of a model of numerous variations of identical or analogous features accompanied by wide-ranging structural similarities. This is, although Holenstein himself does not use that term, a fractal interpretation of cultural diversity.

Taking up Holenstein's distinction of three levels as our springboard, we can now formulate the key idea of a fractal interpretation of religious diversity:

- *Inter-religious level:* the diversity among religions (different types, patterns and typical elements).
- *Intra-religious level:* replicates as the internal diversity within each of the major traditions.
- *Intra-subjective level:* within common but diverse predispositions of the human mind and psyche.

Let me explain this idea by beginning with a rather simple example. The German phenomenologist of religion Friedrich Heiler had classified the different so-called world religions into two major types: prophetic and mystical religions. Some decades later, Julia Ching and Hans Küng expanded this into a threefold typology, distinguishing prophetic, mystical and sapiential, that is wisdom religions. The prophetic religions, Judaism, Christianity and Islam, are of Semitic origin; mystical religions, that is Hinduism and Buddhism, are of Indian origin; and sapiential religions, Confucianism and Daoism, are of Chinese origin. Each of the three types of religions is marked by a central religious figure, the prophet, the mystic and the sage. But then, Ching and Küng, add an important clause to their classification. Prophetic religions also contain certain elements and features of mystical and of sapiential religions. Mystical religions contain elements and features of prophetic and sapiential religions. And sapiential religions contain elements of prophetic and mystical religions.[22] Astonishingly, Ching and Küng did not pay much attention to this startling observation. Yet what it shows is that religious diversity, as described by these three types of religions, displays a fractal structure. The diversity of prophetic, mystical and sapiential religions is replicated by the internal diversity within each one of them. The pattern of this fractal

---

[22] H. Küng/J. Ching, *Christianity and Chinese Religions* (New York: Doubleday, 1989), 25–26.

A Fractal Interpretation of Religious Diversity

Figure 7. Poincaré chains.

structure matches that of the so-called Poincaré chains (see fig. 7).[23]

Phenomenologists of religion had come fairly close to the discovery of fractal patterns. Broadly speaking, the phenomenology of religion pursued two different aims: at the interreligious level, they created typologies of different religions, and at the intrareligious level, they developed typologies of the different elements or components within the religions. The overall expectation was to find strong correlations between specific types of religions and the

---

[23] Source of the figure: Mandelbrot, *The Fractal Geometry of Nature*, 173.

respective typical elements. But this was thwarted by the discovery of countless parallels in and among the religions at the level of elements and components which did not correspond to the expectation of identifying clear-cut differences.

An early phenomenologist who anticipated a fractal understanding of religious diversity was Hilko Wiardo Schomerus. Schomerus distinguished four major types of religions:[24]

a) religions of the law (e.g. Judaism),
b) magical-sacramental religions (e.g. Indian mysticism),
c) gnostic religions (e.g. Greek Gnosis and Buddhism),
d) devotional religions (e.g. Hindu *bhakti*-traditions and some forms of Mahāyāna Buddhism).

Schomerus derived his typology from a traditional Hindu distinction of four different paths of salvation: the way of works (*karma-marga*), the way of meditation (*yoga-marga*), the way of knowledge (*jñana-marga*) and the way of devotion (*bhakti-marga*). However, according to Schomerus, the actual religions cannot be allocated strictly to these four different types: "There are religious formations which comprise not only one of the said four major types but several or even all four of them, and this in a variegated mixture".[25] The fact that Hinduism includes

---

[24] H.W. Schomerus, *Parallelen zum Christentum als religionsgeschichtliches und theologisches Problem* (Gütersloh: Bertelsmann, 1932), 22. The examples in brackets are given by Schomerus.

[25] Ibid., 22 (my translation).

all four types is thus only one example of a more general situation. Hence the distinction between the four types should be applied to the actual religions not vertically but horizontally, even if in some religions one of the four types may exert a dominant and formative influence. How close Schomerus came to a fractal interpretation is obvious when he states: "Religion as such is hypostasized in a few major types, which persistently recur and unfold everywhere in similar ways, bringing about in all places kindred forms and formations".[26]

Let me mention one more, very recent example, that is, James Ford's 2016 comparative study of concepts of the Ultimate in different religious traditions. After discussing such standard contrapositions as 'one versus many', 'personal versus impersonal' or 'transcendent versus immanent' in relation to the Ultimate, Ford arrives at the following conclusion:

> I [...] do not assume that a particular tradition can be characterized by one of the particular poles of these dichotomies. But these dualities do reflect interesting tensions between and within traditions that are worth noting. The heterogeneous nature of these traditions suggests a fluidity that should problematize any essentialized or reified characterizations.[27]

---

[26] Ibid., 26 (my translation).
[27] J.L. Ford, *The Divine Quest, East and West. A Comparative Study of Ultimate Realities* (Albany: SUNY, 2016), 308.

Today we find a large consensus among religious studies scholars about the mixed, hybrid and syncretistic nature of all the major religious traditions. Much more attention is paid to the internal diversity of religions than in the early days of the discipline. We now realise that there is no such thing as true and pure Buddhism, true and pure Islam or true and pure Christianity. To quote Peter van der Veer: "Every religion is syncretistic since it constantly draws upon heterogeneous elements, to the extent that it is often impossible for historians to unravel what comes from where".[28] Or as Tinu Ruparell recently said: "Religious hybridity is simply a fact of the history of religions".[29] However, an important insight that comes with the fractal understanding is that the internal diversity and variety of religions is not entirely arbitrary or purely coincidental. The range of internal religious diversity corresponds rather to the diversity that we find among the religions. To put it succinctly: religions are neither all the same, nor are they completely different. Religions resemble each other precisely in their internal diversity, although the various aspects of this diversity are differently arranged in each one of them.

---

[28] P. van der Veer, "Syncretism, multiculturalism, and the discourse of tolerance", in C. Stewart/R. Shaw (ed.), *Syncretism/Anti-Syncretism. The Politics of Religious Synthesis* (London/New York: Routledge, 1994) 196–211, on p. 208.

[29] T. Ruparell, "Interreligious Dialogue and Interstitial Theology", in C. Cornille (ed.), *The Wiley-Blackwell Companion to Inter-Religious Dialogue* (Oxford: Wiley-Blackwell, 2013) 117–132, on p. 117.

A Fractal Interpretation of Religious Diversity

So what, then, about the third level, that is, the intra-subjective level? On this level the fractal configuration can be analysed both transcendentally and psychologically. It was in particular Rudolph Otto who concluded that the huge number of interreligious parallels should ultimately be explained by the "underlying congruent and common predisposition of humanity in general",[30] which Otto understood as an innate feature of the human mind. Otto assumed a transcendental foundation that accounts for the possibility not merely of religious experience as such but also for its different forms. The assumption that basic patterns of religious diversity are rooted in common features and transcendental structures of the human mind can also be interpreted in terms of religious psychology. An early proponent of this perspective was William James, who suggested a psychological correspondence between the diversity of religions and the diversity of different types of religious personalities as they are found within each religion.[31] Yet it is not only different personalities who, at the intra-subjective level, represent different forms of religion. There is also plenty of evidence that one and the same person may instantiate different forms of religion in the course of his or her own life, as has,

---

[30] "[...] die zugrundeliegende, einheitliche, gemeinsame Anlage der Menschheit überhaupt"; see R. Otto, *Vischnu-Nārāyana. Texte zur indischen Gottesmystik* (Jena: Eugen Diederichs, 1923), 217; see also ibid., 222.
[31] W. James, *The Varieties of Religious Experience* (New York: Vintage Books, 1990 [1st edn; 1902]), 436–438.

for example, been shown by James Fowler[32] and other psychologists.

Finally, there is also the possibility that different religious options may co-inhabit the psyche of a single individual person simultaneously. This takes us to the phenomenon of multi-religious identity and multi-religious belonging. In her profound study of multi-religious belonging, Rose Drew notes that individuals who consciously follow two different religions in fact often oscillate between the two different perspectives, which are not always easily synthesised.[33] This observation has been confirmed by another study on dual-belonging, which describes the spiritual attitude of so-called JuBus, that is Jewish-Buddhists, as a "perpetually ongoing inner dialogue".[34] Drew concludes that in this kind of internalised spiritual dialogue, dual-belongers "become microcosms of the dialogue as a whole".[35] This connects the smallest level of religious diversity with the largest one and matches a fractal interpretation. In a sense, it still follows the pattern of the Poincaré chains.

---

[32] This observation does not require one to accept the evolutionary and hierarchical model that Fowler proposed, see J. Fowler, *Stages of Faith, The Psychology of Human Development and the Quest for Meaning* (San Francisco: Harper & Row, 1981).

[33] R. Drew, *Buddhist and Christian? An Exploration of Dual Belonging* (London: Routledge, 2011), 209ff.

[34] M. Niculescu, "I the Jew, I the Buddhist. Multi-Religious Belonging as Inner Dialogue" *Crosscurrents* 62, 3 (2012), 350–359, on p. 356.

[35] Drew, *Buddhist and Christian?*, 226.

Let me now move on from intercultural philosophy and comparative religion to what I call 'interreligious theology'. Whereas comparative studies have significantly declined within religious studies in favour of localised case studies, interreligious comparison has seen a strong revival in the context of interreligious dialogue and its theological reflection.[36] As I shall show, it is here that a fractal view of religious diversity acquires particular significance.

3. *Interreligious Theology and the Fractal View of Religious Diversity*

By interreligious theology I understand a way of practicing theology which is still rooted within one particular religious tradition but is convinced that relevant truth is also found in other religious traditions. Interreligious theology therefore draws on other religions when reflecting on major questions of human life in order to reconsider, and further develop, the answers that have been given by one's own tradition in a fresh comparative light. In addition, it will reflect on one's own tradition in order to find out which possible contribution can be made from the wealth of this tradition to the issues on the agenda of a global interreligious theological inquiry. Hence interreligious theology is a process of both 'give and take'.

---

[36] See P. Schmidt-Leukel/A. Nehring (ed.), *Interreligious Comparisons in Religious Studies and Theology. Comparison Revisited* (London/New York: Bloomsbury Academic, 2016).

In more recent years, we have seen a steady increase of theological works along the lines of interreligious theology as just described. Several of these works have come across certain phenomena which are best described in terms of fractals. Let me mention three examples. John Cobb, Mark Heim and Bhikkhu Buddhadāsa have each suggested a classification of religious diversity which implies fractal structures.

Cobb distinguishes three different types of religions: cosmic, acosmic and theistic.[37]

Each of these three types correlates with a specific concept of ultimate reality and a corresponding set of religious experiences. That is, cosmic concepts of ultimate reality recognise a sacred nature of the cosmos itself, as, for example, in Daoism or Native American religions. They correspond to experiences which suggest "a kind of belonging to the cosmos, or kinship with other creatures, about which ordinary experience does not inform us".[38] The Mahāyāna-Buddhist concept of emptiness (*śūnyatā*) or the Advaita-Vedāntic concept of Brahman without attributes (*nirguṇa brahman*) are taken by Cobb as examples of acosmic concepts of the ultimate.[39] They correspond to experiences of "a removal of all culturally and existentially

---

[37] For a summary of Cobb's views see D.R. Griffin, "John Cobb's Whiteheadian Complementary Pluralism", in D.R. Griffin (ed.), *Deep Religious Pluralism* (Louisville: Westminster John Knox Press, 2005) 39–66.

[38] J.B. Cobb, *Transforming Christianity and the World. A Way beyond Absolutism and Relativism*, ed. by P. Knitter (Maryknoll, N.Y.: Orbis, 1999), 117.

[39] Griffin, *Deep Religious Pluralism*, 47.

determined barriers to openness to what is as it is", or the discovery of an "inward" nature, "of a 'depth' that is free from all the particularities of ordinary experience".[40] Theistic concepts, finally, correspond to experiences of a personal presence, of communion, of guidance, of being called to a life of righteousness and love and of being released from guilt.[41] According to Cobb these different concepts are not related to different experiences of one and the same ultimate reality, but refer to different ultimates or, better, to ontologically different, but still ultimate, features of one complex reality. However, I shall not discuss Cobb's metaphysics here.

It is a different aspect to which I would like to draw your attention. Cobb developed his classification of cosmic, acosmic and theistic religions under the influence of John A. Hutchison.[42] And like Hutchison himself, Cobb makes, more or less in passing, the interesting observation that "more than one of these types can be discerned in most of the great traditions".[43] That is, Cobb uses his typology in both ways: to classify different religious traditions *and* to classify different manifestations within each of the religious traditions. In other words, Cobb applies a

---

[40] Cobb, *Transforming Christianity and the World*, 118.
[41] Ibid.
[42] Ibid., 120 (Cobb refers to the second edition of Hutchison's *Paths of Faiths* of 1975). Hutchison, however, speaks of cosmic, acosmic and historical religion and is influenced in his terminology by Mircea Eliade.
[43] Cobb, *Transforming Christianity and the World*, 121. See J.A. Hutchison, *Paths of Faith* (4th edn; Boston: McGraw-Hill, 1991), 17.

fractal interpretation of religious diversity and he interprets major features of this diversity as complementary.

My second example is taken from Mark Heim who is a major figure in current debates about the theology of religions. Mark Heim is a Christian inclusivist. He holds that the Trinitarian concept of Christianity provides the best and most comprehensive description of ultimate reality. Furthermore, he interprets other concepts of the ultimate as entailing different aspects of the Trinity. According to Heim, the Trinity comprises three dimensions: an impersonal dimension, a personal or iconic dimension and a communion dimension.

These three dimensions are mirrored in different types of religions and their specific concepts of the ultimate. The impersonal dimension of the Trinity consists in the mutual indwelling of the three persons. That is, each person is completely one with the other two persons and therefore totally empty of itself. The latter aspect of this dimension is, according to Heim, reflected in Buddhist 'not-self' teachings and in concepts like *nirvāṇa* or 'emptiness', while the former aspect of radical mutual indwelling is mirrored in non-dual concepts of the ultimate, most clearly so in Advaita Vedānta. The personal or iconic dimension of the Trinity consists in that "the three constitute one will, one purpose, one love toward creation".[44] This dimension is at

---

[44] S.M. Heim, "The Depth of the Riches: Trinity and Religious Ends", in V. Mortensen (ed.), *Theology and the Religions. A Dialogue* (Grand Rapids/Cambridge: Eerdmans, 2003) 387–402, on p. 394.

the center of monotheistic concepts of the ultimate, but it is also present in the perception of a divine law without a divine person, as in Daoism or in classical Stoicism: "What is apprehended in these cases is the external unity of the Trinity",[45] appearing as one divine or heavenly will or law. The third dimension, that is the communion dimension, underlies the other two dimensions. It combines unity and difference in that the three persons participate and share in each other,[46] comparable to human relationships of "deep love or intimate friendship".[47]

Like Cobb, Heim makes the interesting observation that "each great religious tradition in some measure recognizes the variety of dimensions we have described", and each grasps "the set of dimensions *through* one of them".[48] Obviously, this implies a fractal perspective, for Heim suggests that the differences between various types of religions are also present within each one of them. He even admits that 'formally' Christianity is not different from other religions.[49] That is, Christianity, too, apprehends all three dimensions through the lens of one dimension which is taken as dominant, in that case, the dimension of communion.

My third and final example comes from the Thai Buddhist reformer Bhikkhu Buddhadāsa. According to

---

[45] Ibid., 396.
[46] Ibid., 397.
[47] Ibid., 391.
[48] Ibid., 399.
[49] Ibid.

Buddhadāsa the fundamental means of achieving liberation comprise wisdom, faith and will power.

They are not only found in Buddhism but also in Christianity, Islam and Hinduism, though with different emphases and in different forms.[50] Buddhism puts its emphasis on wisdom, Christianity on faith, and Islam on will-power. But these three central spiritual qualities form an inner unity, so that, despite the differences, all three are present in each of the three religions: "Each religion comprises all three ways; the only difference is that a certain religion may give preference to one way or the other".[51] Doctrinal differences between the religions are explained by Buddhadāsa as a result of their exposure to different cultural influences.[52] In order to support this view, Buddhadāsa drew not on a Buddhist authority but, interestingly, on the Qur'ān's affirmation that there is a messenger for each nation (10:47).[53]

As my examples illustrate, the discovery of fractal structures in the diversity of religions does not depend on one particular and specific form of typology. My impression is that whatever scheme we choose in depicting, demarcating and analysing religious diversity, we shall come across fractal patterns. Thus I propose a fractal interpretation of

---

[50] B.I. Buddhadāsa, *Christianity and Buddhism. Sinclaire Thompson Memorial Lecture, Fifth Series* (Bangkok: Sublime Life Mission, 1967), 12ff, 24f, 38f.
[51] Ibid., 13.
[52] Ibid., 24f.
[53] Ibid., 8.

religious diversity in a heuristic, almost pragmatic sense. It should encourage us not to view religions as static and homogenous entities but to face their internal diversity and hybridity while at the same time looking for analogous forms of diversity and hybridity within one's own tradition. This way of perceiving religious diversity will be extremely fruitful in relation to the aim of carrying out theology interreligiously.

4. *The Fruitfulness of the Theory*

In 1870, Max Müller, the well-known pioneer of comparative [religion], famously stated: "Anyone who knows this [religion i.e. Christianity] knows all".[54] About three decades later, the German theologian Adolf von Harnack replied with the words: "Whoever knows this religion [Christianity] knows them all".[55] While these two statements

---

[54] "When the students of Comparative Philology boldly adapted Goethe's paradox, 'He who possesses one language, knows none,' people were startled at first; but they soon began to feel the truth which was hidden beneath the paradox. [...] The same applies to religion. He who knows one, knows none". See M. Müller, *Einleitung in die vergleichende Religionswissenschaft* (2nd edn; Strassburg: Karl J. Tübner, 1876), 21-22. The quotation is from a lecture that Müller held in 1870.

[55] "Wer diese Religion nicht kennt, kennt keine und wer sie samt ihrer Geschichte kennt, kennt alle". ("Anyone who does not know this religion [i.e. Christianity] knows no religion and anyone who knows this [religion i.e. Christianity] including its history knows all [religions]".); A. von Harnack, *Die Aufgabe der theologischen Fakultäten und die allgemeine Religionsges-*

appear to be, at first sight, irreconcilable, a fractal interpretation of religious diversity shows that both of them are, to some extent, correct. The fractal structures which we can discern in religious diversity are not those of the strict self-similarity as in the Sierpinski triangle. They are, rather, similar to the irregular forms of self-similarity as in coast lines. Some religions are like large bays, others like fiords and still others like spits. Yet if we look at them more closely, we find that the coast line of the large bay includes small fiords and spits or we discover that there are small bays and fiords in the coast lines of spits. The irregularity is one in terms of different emphases, different arrangements and different contexts. Hence this is what enables the religions to learn from each other. The other religion is always different but never wholly other. Thus Müller was right to argue that one needs to learn about many different religions in order to achieve a better understanding of each one of them. And Harnack was also right to see that what is found in other religions is also present, although in different ways, in one's own religion. However, he was wrong to assume that this is only true for Christianity.

The discovery of a correspondence between inter-religious diversity and intra-religious diversity shows that there is far more continuity between ecumenical theology and interreligious theology than people usually assume.

chichte (vol. 2 of *Reden und Aufsätze*, Gießen: Töppelmann, 1901), 159–187, on p. 168.

This implies, among other things, that one's attitude to the religious other will be interconnected with one's attitude to the denominational or spiritual other within one's own religious tradition. There is a bond between what one could call the small and the large ecumenism. Yet the implication of a fractal interpretation of religious diversity goes still deeper. It suggests that central doctrinal concepts are not only interrelated with other concepts of their own doctrinal schemes. It also assumes that they are multifaceted because they are subject to a variety of interpretations within the various contexts of different sub-traditions or schools within one and the same religious tradition. Because this applies to each of major traditions, it will always be possible to seek and discern interlinks with some facets of related concepts from other religious traditions. And this explains why interreligious theology carries the promise of reciprocal illumination.

Let me explain such fractal interrelations between religious concepts by means of three confessional categories: the *Buddha*, that is, the 'Awakened One'; the *Son*, that is the 'Incarnation of God', and the *Prophet* as the 'Seal of Revelation'.

Gautama, under the Bo-Tree, *awakens* to the ultimate refuge from suffering, Nirvāṇa, and, out of compassion, *proclaims* the way he had found thereby *embodying* Nirvāṇa and Dharma.

Jesus, in the desert, *awakens* to the ultimate source of life, God, and, in subsequently reflecting, imitating and *proclaiming* God's mercy he *embodies* the eternal word of life.

Muhammad, in the wilderness of the mountain, *awakens* to the ultimate unity of true reality, and out of divine commission, *proclaims* God's oneness, justice and mercy thereby *embodying* both, the eternal word of God in his message and, in his life, submission to God as the essence of all reality.

Thus in Gautama, Jesus and Muhammad we find an aspect of awakening and prophetic ministry which their followers, retrospectively, understood as the two facets of embodying or incarnating ultimate reality.

Through interreligious theology, Muslims may therefore discover that, and how, prophethood also involves the dimensions of incarnation and of awakening. The prophet is someone in whom the Word of God assumes an earthly incarnation in the form of the prophet's divine message. Even more so, a human being can become a prophet – without ceasing to be human – only if the potential or seed of being a prophet is somehow part of the human nature to which a particular human being awakens. The Muslim concept of a prophet-reality or Muhammad-reality in every being thus carries strong analogies to the Buddhist understanding of Buddha nature, as has been pointed out by Izutsu Toshihiko and by Reza Shah-Kazemi.[56] Conversely, Buddhists might become better aware that the way to

---

[56] T. Izutsu, *The Structure of Oriental Philosophy: Collected Papers of the Eranos Conference* (2 vol.; Tokyo: Keio University Press, 2008), 170f and R. Shah-Kazemi, *Common Ground Between Islam and Buddhism* (Louisville: Fons Vitae, 2010), 59f, 72.

Buddhahood may also include the quality of a prophetic voice (as is particularly evident in the case of Nichiren) and that the incarnational dimension of Buddha nature may justly assume theistic forms, as it actually often did in the Buddhist tradition. Christians can recognise and appreciate the incarnational dimension of awakening and rediscover that, and how, incarnational thinking is rooted in prophetic revelation. Jesus can thus be seen as the one in whom the divine word assumed not just the form of a message but that of a whole life, which itself became the message. Hence even central religious categories like that of the Prophet, the Son and the Buddha show a fractal sub-structure: each contains in itself components of the other two. But it does so in a way which invites processes of mutual learning or reciprocal illumination.

The Controversial Image of Moses in Rabbinic Literature

Lieve Teugels

In the Jewish tradition, Moses is undoubtedly the least disputed leader and the main spiritual ancestor of the Jewish people. *Moshe rabbenu* has become the epitome of leadership in Judaism up to the present day, even outside Judaism. In the Netherlands, my colleague Marcel Poorthuis has just published a book which transfers the story of Moses to the situation of the bankers and managers of the Amsterdam business centre: *Managing with Moses*.[1] This is only one of such books; there are many more.

On the tomb of the great twelfth century Jewish leader and philosopher Moses Maimonides, in Tiberias, one can read the inscription: "From Moses to Moses, no one like Moses stood up".

The same adage was used, somewhat adapted, with respect to the leader of Jewish enlightenment in the eighteenth century, Moses Mendelsohn, in the journal

---

[1] M. Poorthuis, *Managen met Mozes. Lessen uit de woestijn voor leiders van vandaag* (Amsterdam: Pardes, 2017).

Ha-meassef,[2] where you can read that "from Moses to Moses there was no one wise like Moses". Like Moses Maimonides, Moses Mendelsohn was a Bible scholar and a philosopher, and just like the biblical Moses, Mendelsohn was apparently a stutterer. To be a Jewish leader, therefore, it helps if your parents gave you the name Moses,[3] yet this is not evident because Moses was not born a natural leader.

In this presentation I want to look, albeit briefly, at some biblical texts, then move on to an early rabbinic biblical commentary, a midrash from about the third century CE, and finally to a somewhat later rabbinic text, from the Babylonian Talmud.

In the book of Exodus, Moses is depicted as a remarkably human figure, with occasionally low self-esteem and doubts about his suitability as a leader. This already starts in Exodus Chapters 3 and 4, even at the burning bush.

In Exodus 3:11, we read: "Who am I that I should go to Pharaoh and free the Israelites from Egypt?". In 4:1: "What if they do not believe me and do not listen to me, but say: The Lord did not appear to you?". And in 4:10: "Please, O Lord, I have never been a man of words, either in times past or now that You have spoken to Your servant;

---

[2] *Ha-meassef* 2 (1785), 81.
[3] René Bloch, however, states that the name Moses was explicitly not given to Jewish boys until late antiquity, apparently out of respect. See R. Bloch, "Entre grandeur et humanité, Moïse dans le judaïsme ancien", *Le monde de la Bible*, 2015, issue *Figures de Moïse: Les différentes facettes d'un personnage*, 29–47, on p. 31, e-book.

I am slow of speech and slow of tongue". Finally, in v. 13: "Please, O Lord, make someone else Your agent".

In Exodus 4:12 and 14, we read that God loses his patience and becomes angry with Moses, which is, it would seem, not a good start for a great leader. Yet Moses is considered an example for all leadership. How did that come to be?

If we look at the earliest rabbinic midrashim, we see that they depict Moses in an equally ambivalent way and they even magnify his doubtful leadership qualities. I have selected a typical text that concerns Moses' dubious authority, especially his ambivalent relationship with God. This text pertains to Moses' calling at the burning bush but it connects this to Moses' last hours, particularly to the question as to why Moses was not allowed to enter the land of Israel. A specific feature of this midrash is that it contains a parable (*mashal*). Parables in midrash, as in other contexts, are excellent ways of narrating difficult things in an indirect way. This is the parable, in its midrashic context, as it appears in *Mekhilta de Rabbi Shimon bar Yohai*, tractate Sanya, to Exodus 4:13.[4]

---

[4] The translation of the following text is taken from my forthcoming annotated edition: L.M. Teugels, *The Parables in Mekhilta de Rabbi Ishmael and Mekhilta de Rabbi Shimon bar Yochai: A Critical Edition with Translation and Commentary* (Tübingen: Mohr Siebeck, 2018); the critical edition of Mekhilta de Rabbi Ishmael is: J.N. Epstein/E.Z. Melamed (ed.), *Mekhilta d'rabbi Sim'on b. Jochai. Fragmenta in Geniza Cairensa reperta digessit apparatu critico, notis, praedatione instruxit* (Jerusalem: Mekitse Nirdamim, 1955).

Therefore, the Holy One, blessed be He, pressed Moses for six days and on the seventh he said to Him: "Make someone else Your agent!" (Exod 4:13). As it says: "But Moses said to the Lord, 'Please, Lord, I am not a man (of words)'" (Exod 4:10).

They told this parable. To what is the matter similar? To a king who had a servant and he loved him with a complete love. And the king sought to make him his administrator, to take care of the maintenance of the members of the king's palace. What did that king do? He took the servant by his hand and brought him into his treasury and showed him silver vessels and golden vessels, fine stones and gems and all that he had in his treasury. After this, he brought him outside and showed him trees, gardens, orchards and enclosed areas, and all that he had in the fields. Afterwards, the servant closed his hand and said: "I cannot be made administrator to take care of the maintenance of the members of the king's palace". The king said to him: "If you could not be made administrator, why did you put me through all this trouble?". And the king was angry at him and decreed over him that he should not enter his palace.

So the Holy One, blessed be He, pressed Moses for six days and on the seventh he said to Him: "Make someone else Your agent!" (Exod 4:13). The Holy One, blessed be He, swore over him that he would not enter the land of Israel. As is said: "(Because you did not trust Me enough to affirm my sanctity in the sight of the Israelite people), therefore you shall not lead (this congregation into the land that I have given them)" (Num 20:12).

The Controversial Image of Moses in Rabbinic Literature

A very brief preliminary word about rabbinic parables may be required.⁵ As a rule, a rabbinic parable consists of two parts, the parable proper, called *mashal*; and its application, called *nimshal*. Both are introduced with stereotypical formulae, which I have marked in italic type in the text for easy recognition. Since the parable is part of a midrash, the biblical verse, or verses, that are the focus of the commentary are quoted first. We call this the base text: in this case this is Exodus 4:10-13. Frequently, as in this case, there is a piece of midrash before the *mashal*. The *mashal* is, as a rule, a fictional story, usually with stereotypical characters such as a king (who stands for God), and his son, or his servant (who in this case, stands for Moses). The *nimshal*, the application, brings the focus back to the biblical base text, as is also the case here.

The base text, Exodus 4:10-13, is quoted in the beginning of the passage. Because of the repeated hesitations of Moses, the midrash concludes that God had been pressing Moses for six days. This is not stated in the Bible: this is typical midrashic gap-filling.⁶ The comparison in the

---

⁵ About rabbinic parables, see, most prominently: D. Stern, *Parables in Midrash: Narrative and Exegesis in Rabbinic Literature* (Cambridge, Mass.: Harvard University Press, 1991); Y. Fraenkel, "Hamashal", in *Darkhe ha-aggadah vehamidrash* (2 vol.; Givataim: Yad letalmud, 1991) 323-393.

⁶ D. Boyarin, *Intertextuality and the Reading of Midrash* (Bloomington: Indiana University Press, 1990), passim; L.M. Teugels, "Gap Filling and Linkage in the Midrash on the Rebekah Cycle", in A. Wénin (ed.), *Studies in the Book of Genesis. Literature, Redaction and History* (Leuven: Peeters, 2001) 585-598.

mashal is quite straightforward: Moses is compared to a beloved servant who is chosen by the king to administer his household but, after a tour of the property, refuses to take up the task because he "cannot do it". The king is angry because he has put in time and effort to prepare the servant for the job. Therefore, he forbids the servant to enter his palace.

In the *nimshal*, this is reverted again to the relationship between God and Moses. Because Moses initially refuses to be God's agent (Exod 4:13), he will not be allowed to enter the land.

The interpretation offered by the *mashal*, and especially the *nimshal*, adds something to the biblical text: in the Bible, Moses' initial refusal to be the representative of his people is never adduced as the reason why he will not be allowed to enter the land. Rather, other reasons are given, such as Moses' (ambiguous) reaction to the people in Numbers 20:10, when he is about to strike a rock to bring out water on God's command, and says: "Listen, you rebels, shall we get water for you out of this rock?". God's reaction to this in Numbers 20:12 is quoted at the end of our text: "Because you did not trust Me enough to affirm my sanctity in the sight of the Israelite people, therefore you shall not lead this congregation into the land that I have given them" (Num 20:12). Thus, the midrash connects Numbers 20:10–12 with the situation in Exodus 4, whereas in the biblical text these events are unrelated. This is again the typical gap-filling and linking of passages that we often find in rabbinic midrash.

The fact that Moses was never allowed to enter the land of Israel is a major issue in rabbinic midrash. It is

The Controversial Image of Moses in Rabbinic Literature

consistently argued that this was very disappointing for Moses. This probably teaches us more about the rabbis who composed these commentaries than about Moses himself. It is evident that the ancient rabbis, who saw Moses as their great leader, found this a very harsh decision on the part of God; they saw it as an ordeal that Moses had not deserved. Thus, the midrash relates *at nauseum* how Moses begged God to change His plan, and offered various alternatives, such as to let him enter through a tunnel, or in disguise, or even as a dead body in a coffin.[7] But God did not give in.

How does the rabbinic tradition make sense of the two facts that are addressed in this midrash: first, that Moses was initially very reluctant to be a leader; second, that he was not allowed to enter the land? As we have seen, in the earliest rabbinic commentaries, these two events are connected: *because* he first refused to be a leader, he was not allowed to enter. This is a different reason than the one given in the Bible: there it is said that he was not allowed to go in because he was angry with the people, and because he claimed ownership of a miracle, whereas in fact only God can work miracles. None of this is found the tannaitic midrashim: they present him as a very human and humble, even insecure, leader who does not receive the reward he had so much hoped for: to enter the land. In his recent book about Moses in the rabbinic tradition, Günter Stemberger explains this in the following way:

---

[7] See, for example, Sifre, to Numbers, Piska 341, Num 32:52.

> The image of the leadership of Moses is not only based on the biblical image, but also on the presuppositions of the rabbis about how an ideal leader of the Jewish community should act. Because these were themselves usually not yet in a leadership position, they were interested in a conciliatory, service-minded community leader, who does not become angry, who does not follow his own interests, who is not authoritarian. All this may have played on the background of the passive image that Moses has in rabbinic literature.[8]

In later rabbinic literature, notably in the Babylonian Talmud, we see that this passive, even suffering, image receives a very specific interpretation. In tractate Sotah, the place of Moses' death, *and* the fact that he was not allowed to go in, are read as manifestations of the biblical prophecy of the suffering servant of Isaiah 53. Moses is presented as the one who suffered to atone for the sins of his people.

> R. Hama son of R. Hanina also said: "Why was Moses buried near Beth-peor? To atone for the incident at Peor" (see Numbers 25).
> [...]
> R. Simlai expounded: "Why did Moses our teacher yearn to enter the land of Israel? Did he want to eat of its fruits or satisfy himself from its bounty?". But thus spoke

---

[8] G. Stemberger, *Mose in der rabbinischen Tradition* (Freiburg: Herder, 2016), 184–185.

The Controversial Image of Moses in Rabbinic Literature

Figure 1. Ludovico Carracci, *Transfiguration*, oil on canvas, Bologna, Pinacoteca Nazionale, 1595-1596 (With the permission of the Ministry of Cultural Heritage and Activities, Polo museale dell'Emilia Romagna).

> Moses, "Many precepts were commanded to Israel which can only be fulfilled in the land of Israel. I wish to enter the land so that they may all be fulfilled by me". The Holy One, blessed be He, said to him, "Is it only to receive the reward for obeying the commandments that you seek? I ascribe it to you as if you did perform them"; as it is said: "Therefore will I divide him a portion with the great, and he shall divide the spoil with the strong; because he poured out his soul unto death, and was numbered with the transgressors; yet he bore the sins of many, and made intercession for the transgressors" (Isaiah 53:12). [...] "Because he poured out his soul unto death" – because he surrendered himself to die, as it is said "Now, if You will forgive their sin [well and good]; but if not, erase me from the record which You have written!" (Exod 32:32) "And was numbered with the transgressors" – because he was numbered with them who were condemned to die in the wilderness. "Yet he bore the sins of many" – because he secured atonement for the making of the Golden Calf. "And made intercession for the transgressors" – because he begged for mercy on behalf of the sinners in Israel that they should turn in penitence.[9]

Even though there is no proof, this presentation of Moses seems to be a reaction to the Christian application of this text to Jesus, as in Luke 22:27 and Hebrews 9:28.[10]

---

[9] BT Sotah 14a (Soncino translation).
[10] Cf. Stemberger, *Mose in der rabbinischen*, 184–185.

The Controversial Image of Moses in Rabbinic Literature

To summarise our topic so far: Moses entered Jewish history as *moshe rabbenu*, but this does not mean that the classical rabbinic texts present him as an infallible leader. Quite the contrary: they seem to emphasise that a leader can be human and must be compassionate rather than authoritarian.

It must, however, be said that there are certain strands in Jewish interpretation, even very early ones, that present him differently. In the Hellenistic Jewish texts, Moses is often pictured as an almost divine figure, who did not die but was "taken up in heaven", and sat on a throne next to God.[11] This image is also found in Christian views of Moses, who is presented next to Elijah at Jesus' transfiguration, as in the painting by Ludovico Carracci that is displayed in the Pinacoteca Nazionale of Bologna (fig. 1). It seems likely that the rabbinic line of interpretation, which became the most influential strand in Jewish thought up until the present day, was a reaction to this Hellenistic and Christian quasi-divinization of Moses, and also to the Christian interpretations of Jesus, who is, on the one hand, identified with the suffering servant, and, on the other, presented as a divine saviour.

---

[11] See e.g. P.W. Horst, "Moses' Throne Vision in Ezekiel the Dramatist", *Journal of Jewish Studies* 34, 1 (1983) 21–30.

Martin Luther, the Eleutherius: The Freedom of Intended Ambiguity of Theology and Gender

Else Marie Wiberg Pedersen

1. *Introduction*

In this paper, I shall highlight Martin Luther's views on women and gender pertaining to theology and ministry. I will do so seeing Luther in his own sixteenth-century context, avoiding any judgement of him according to our twenty-first-century norms and standards. One of my points will be that – despite all the faults and failures of Luther, as a human being – it is possible to extrapolate and highlight features of his theology that eventually led to political and social improvements for women since such features were intended for all common people irrespective of sex, ethnicity, and social background.

During recent decades, Luther's legacy as a Reformer pertaining to the status of women has been questioned. Some feminist scholars, such as historian Merry Wiesner-Hanks, have claimed that whether scholars carry out feminist studies and whether they are negative or positive towards Luther's legacy concern confessional and/or national biases. Thus, Wiesner-Hanks has made the claim that German female scholars are less prone to be critical of Luther than non-German, particularly American, female scholars.[1] Although such a statement may be simplifying the matter, there is much truth in the claim that how we read Luther has to do with our confessional and national biases. It is probably not surprising for us to find more positive voices on the Lutheran side, such as Steve Ozment, Roland Bainton, or Kirsi Stjerna,[2] albeit in a critical reading. On the other hand, the most critical voices raised against Luther's impact on women's lives, denying any positive effect, are not neutral feminist scholars, either. Most are Anglo-American feminists with a Catholic or Anglican background.[3]

The Reformer's viewpoint concerning women and gender has, indeed, been one of the most widely debated themes regarding the Reformation's impact on theology, church and society. Feminists and/or scholars of modernity have criticised Luther for causing anything but a reformation of gender roles, maintaining that women's place in

---

[1] M. Wiesner-Hanks, "Women and the Reformations: Reflections on Recent Research", in *History Compass* 2 (2 vol.; Wiley online library, 2004) 1–27.

[2] S. Ozment, *When Fathers Ruled. Family life in Reformation Europe* (Cambridge, Mass.: Harvard University Press, 1985), 54ff; R. Bainton, *Women in the Reformation of Germany and Italy* (Minneapolis: Fortress press, 1971); K. Stjerna, *Women and Reformation* (Oxford: Blackwell, 2008).

[3] R. Radford Ruether, *Sexism and God Talk. Towards a Feminist Theology* (Boston: Beacon Press, 1983); M. Wiesner, *Working Women in Renaissance Germany* (New Brunswick: Rutgers University Press, 1986); L. Roper, *The Holy Household* (Oxford: Clarendon Press, 1989). Lately, also representatives from Radical Orthodoxy, such as Sarah Coakley.

society at large deteriorated. The critics particularly contend that Luther's opposition to monasticism and virginity as a holy ideal, in tandem with his re-evaluation of Mary as a real woman rather than a saint, sparked a backlash for the esteem and value of women. One claim is that, since Luther and the other reformers valued marriage higher than the celibacy of monks and nuns, women's career opportunities were reduced to those of becoming wives and mothers, men alone gaining from the new societal arrangements.[4] Lyndal Roper has been claiming this since 1989 based on her research into the civic positions in Augsburg, and it has been repeated by several others resistant to in-depth research into Luther's own text corpus, not acknowledging theology as a positive game changer.[5] Another claim is that Luther's new understanding of the ecclesial office as an integral part of the priesthood of all believers did not improve women's place in church and

---

[4] L. Roper, *The Holy Household* and L. Roper, *Martin Luther. Renegade and Prophet* (New York: Penguin Random House, 2017).

[5] The first to make a more nuanced, in-depth analysis of Luther's texts pertaining to women were G. Scharffenorth/K. Thraede, "Freunde in Christus werden...", in *Die Beziehung von Mann und Frau als Frage an Theologie und Kirche* (Berlin: Burckhardtshaus-Verlag, 1977) but this was not considered by Roper. In 1991, Roper's work was critically commented by A. Classen/T.A. Settle, "Women in Martin Luther's Life and Theology", *German Studies Review* 14 (1991) 231–260. The latter studied Luther's letters and the Table Talks, concluding that Luther's view of women was complex and that "Luther did not pursue particular misogynist ideas and was in truth rather modern and open in his approach to women" on p. 254.

society. Conversely, Luther's contemporary opponents accused him of opening avenues for women to circumvent set gender norms by speaking in public. In fact, one of the 41 errors for which Luther was condemned by the Catholic magisterium in 1520, and banned by Emperor Charles V in 1521, was that of even regarding women as better priests than the bishops or the pope.[6] From then on, 'Luther' and its derivative 'Lutheran' were not proper names, but figures of speech that conveyed and denoted dissent, transgression and freedom. Luther even made his name into a trope by signing early letters as the Eleutherius.[7]

In his endeavour to reform the theology and church of his days, Luther totally reformulated the doctrine on ecclesial offices. In this enterprise, his principles of *sola scriptura* and *solus Christus* played a decisive part. Claiming the free right for every Christian to interpret the Bible, and Christ incarnated in his radical humanity, and the word of God as the only authority of the church, Luther subverted the understanding of church and its ministry. Luther thus rejected the ontological difference and hierarchy of power between lay and ordained priests as taught by the papal church, and recast church ministry as a reciprocal and symbiotic relation between the priest ordained to preach the word of God (*ministerium verbi*) and those truly

---

[6] H. Denzinger/A. Schönmetzer (ed.), *Enchiridion symbolorum*, no. 1463.
[7] See R. Buchwald, "Martinus Eleutherius", *Deutsche Monatsschrift* (1912) 421–424; V. Westhelle, *Transfiguring Luther: The Planetary Promise of Luther's Theology* (Eugene, Oregon: Cascade Books, 2016), 197.

ordained through baptism to the priesthood of all believers (*sacerdotes*). In this paper, I wish to show how Luther's radical incarnation theology, with its focus on Christ as a human being, inevitably led to the humanisation of church ministry. This together with his empowering of laypersons, opened avenues for women to see themselves as equal authorities on reading and teaching Scriptures and preaching the word of God. Luther, indeed, held that women could do so in emergency situations when there was no competent man present, such as in convents. Otherwise, he seemed to maintain the norm – as set by Paul in 1 Corinthians 14:34 – that prescribed a male preacher. Yet, when scrutinising Luther's Latin and German texts on this matter, he turns out to be extremely loose in his formulations, even appearing self-contradictory. The significant question then is whether Luther is simply as ambivalent towards women as his predecessors and peers, or whether he chose ambiguity as a theological strategy in the context of a predominantly misogynist, patriarchal society and church. However we interpret Luther, most Lutheran Churches today ordain women pastors, unlike the church that he wanted to reform.

2. *Sola Scriptura, Translation, and Gender*

Even though we can easily find texts where Luther reflects thoughts and rhetoric of traditional exegesis inherited from Augustine and Augustinian tradition, his *sola scriptura* principle in fact goes against a mere traditional way of reading the Scripture. Thus, the Bible humanists' maxim of going to the sources, *ad fontes*, lies at the root of his *sola scriptura* hermeneutic and points to an empowering of every person to read it and see what the Scripture says, taken as gospel, not as a book on law, as Luther explains in his introduction to the German translation of the New Testament.[8]

In his letter of 1530 *On Translation*,[9] the Reformer explains how he endeavoured to renew the German language through his translation of the Bible. Luther explains how a translation cannot simply be a literal rendition and how an extensive vocabulary is required in order to render the content of the original Greek or Hebrew. Translation requires the highest loyalty towards the original, but also industry, patience and a sensitivity in finding the right words.[10] In his struggle to establish a realistic German language, Luther did not merely speak to males. He and his colleagues sought out "the mothers in the house, the children in the streets, and the common man at the market". Women and children were as important as anybody else in his endeavour to renew and recast a feudal society that normally did not value women in general.

It is essential to know that there were very strict rules pertaining to translations and which words were

---

[8] Luther, *Eyn klein Unterricht, was man ynn den Euangeliis suchen und gewarten soll*, WA 10/I, 8–18.
[9] Luther, WA 30/II, 633–634.
[10] Ibid.

admissible. Of particular interest in our context is that Luther decided quite early on to design his translations to be as inclusive as possible. They were to be addressed to the common people, not just to elite males. As a consequence of his thoughts on the Reformation, Luther deviated from tradition when he purposefully replaced Paul's term "sons of God" in Galatians 3:27 and 4:6–7 (plus Rom 8:15 and Matt 5:9) with the term "children of God" in order to incorporate women. Luther was determined to preclude a restriction of God's promises in the Galatians and elsewhere. In the same manner, he decided to replace the term "son of man" with the term "child of humanity" for Christ, central to his rendition of Galatians and of Mary's role in the *Church Postil* of 1522. In another sermon of 1522, *Invocavit Sermon*, Luther interprets Deuteronomy 1:31, "the Lord your God bore you as a man bears his son", by referring to the relation between mother and child:

> I have born and raised you as a mother does with her child: what does she do? First, she gives it milk, then porridge, then eggs and soft food; if she began by giving hard food the child would not thrive. [...] If all mothers rejected their children, where would we be?[11]

Like Bernard of Clairvaux, his great inspiration, Luther was not afraid of cross-gendering his vocabulary when

---

[11] Luther, WA 10/III, 6. All translations into English in this article are my own.

explaining God's caring love.[12] It had both a scriptural foundation and an inclusive and incorporate effect that reflected the equity, sociality and solidarity Luther envisioned as the true way of being a Christian community. Luther is therefore not simply speaking metaphorically. He is also thinking of real mothers and real children, not least all the neglected or abandoned children that he saw in the streets. Children are at the core of how we act as humans and Christians. This is a recurrent concern that is reflected in his imagery, such as in the exposition of the first of the Ten Commandments in his *Large Catechism*, where he calls upon God's commandment to every human to do good to her or his neighbour as a mother feeds her child, for, in the same way as God has provided a mother with breasts and milk to feed her child, every creature is in God's hand, channel and means, Luther asserts.[13] As well as borrowing vocabulary to render his Reform theology in the vernacular, Luther draws on experiences and observations from the world that surrounds him.

Concurrently, just as the extremely important vernacularisation of Scripture is indicative of the empowering of the common people, enabled as they are to read and interpret bible texts on their own, it is imperative for those studying Luther to take the humanist principle of going

---

[12] Luther uses the same *modus operandi* of cross-gendering or playing with set gender roles when addressing his wife, Katharina von Bora, as evidenced in his letters to her.

[13] WA 30/1, 132–139, here on p. 136.

back to the sources seriously. It is not Bible texts alone that may be "lost in translation", misinterpreted and distorted through translation and rendered in different, at times dubious, versions. This is also true of Luther's texts, rendered in many versions as they are. If we do not constantly go back to the sources, we are prone to adopt and render acritically misrepresentations and distortions, deliberate or not, and run the risk of being unable to develop a Lutheran theology in its own right.

3. *Women and Luther's Theology*

An examination of Luther's vast text corpus of more than 100 volumes in the WA shows that Luther's view on women and gender is as complex as his authorship is vast. To us, Luther may sound misogynist when addressing an audience of unmarried priests in scholarly Latin, yet appreciative of women in his annual sermons on matrimony in vernacular German. While seemingly rendering the standard norm of male authority over women, he simultaneously teaches the mutual and equal partnership of women and men that he furthermore practises in his married life with Katharina von Bora from 1525.

4. *Women in the Bible*

Luther's at once complex and fresh views on women is most visible in his sermons and exegetical writings on Bible texts. His exegesis of Genesis 1–3, in particular, reflects the thoughts and rhetoric of traditional exegesis inherited from Augustine onwards, combined with his own fresh readings. In a *Sermon on Genesis* of 1523, Luther, commenting on Genesis 2, stated that Adam was more rational than Eve due to his male nature. With a reference to 1 Timotheus 2:5, Eve is described as a woman representing the weak sex through whom Satan had easy access.[14] In his *Lectures on Genesis* of 1535–1545, Luther seems to have withheld a creational order according to which Adam was more fully the image of God, and remains so after the fall, male to female being like the sun to the moon.[15] Ontologically, Luther at times perceives woman as created for the main purpose of being man's helpmate and of bearing children.

Such perceptions of women, however, were, in the words of Susan Karant-Nunn and Wiesner-Hanks, "hardly original".[16] In fact, Luther here reflects tradition from both the old church and the Middle Ages, and is compatible with most other sixteenth-century theologians.[17] Notwithstanding this, Luther does not simply reflect tradition. He struggles with the traditional and contemporary views of women, finding many of them offensive. He objected to Sebastian Franck's collection of misogynist aphorisms

---

[14] Luther, WA 14, 129–131.
[15] Luther, WA 42, 46.
[16] S. Karant-Nunn/M. Wiesner-Hanks, *Luther on Women. A Sourcebook* (Cambridge: Cambridge University Press, 2003), 16.
[17] For the traditional opinions of women, see e.g. A. Blamires, *The Case for Women in Medieval Culture* (Oxford: Clarendon Press, 1997).

that to his mind were nothing but slanderous of women and destructive for the partnership of men and women.[18] Also, in the very same texts, where Luther proposes the traditional exegesis, he writes extensively more on the positive value of women; not least when he determines the relation between male and female theologically. Moreover, he underlines the equality between Eve and Adam as the image and likeness of God. Theologically, pre-fall Eve is not inferior to Adam, nor is that so eschatologically. Commenting on Genesis 1:27, Luther argues for the equal and independent status of the female sex as *imago Dei* against allegedly Talmudic ideas about the female being cut from a bisexual male, against Aristotle's perception of the woman as an imperfect man, and against the 'gentile' perceptions of the female sex as monsters:

> This tale fits Aristotle's designation of woman as a maimed man; others declare that she is a monster.[19] But let them themselves be monsters and sons of monsters – these men who make malicious statements and ridicule a creature of God in which God took delight as

---

[18] P. Klaus (ed.), *Sprichwörter* (vol. 11 of S. Franck, *Sämtliche Werke: Kritische Ausgabe mit Kommentar*; Bern: Peter Lang, 1993). Cf. Karant-Nunn/Wiesner-Hanks, *Luther on Women*.

[19] "Cum hac fabula convenit, quod Aristoteles appellat mulierem virum occasionatum, et alii monster dicunt". Presumably with reference to his *De generatione animalium*, I, ch. 20, Luther firmly rejects Aristotle's pejorative designation of woman as an imperfect male, *mulierem virum*, as a *fabula*, something made up.

> in a most excellent work, moreover, one which we see created by a special counsel of God. These gentile [pagan] ideas show that reason cannot establish anything sure about God and the works of God but only thinks up reasons against reasons and teaches nothing in a perfect and solid manner.[20]

Pace Luther, such ideas about women, God's most excellent work, are pejorative and most unreasonable. By contrast, Adam and Eve are equal in creation, equally the image and similitude of God, equal recipients of God's word, equally given dominion over the rest of creation, as they have equal future glory.[21]

> Moses puts the two sexes together and says that God created male and female to indicate that Eve, too, was made by God as a partaker of the divine image and of the divine similitude, likewise of the rule over everything. Thus, even today the woman is the partaker of the future life, just as Peter says that they are joint heirs of the same grace (1 Pet 3:7). In the household the wife is a partner in the management and has a common interest in the children and the property, and yet there is a great difference between the sexes.[22]

---

[20] Luther, WA 42, 41–62.
[21] Luther, WA 42, 51.
[22] Luther, WA 42, 41–62.

According to Luther, there is no hierarchy in God's creation of men and women, but there is a difference in the method used. Deliberating on the interpretation of Genesis 2 with the ancient and medieval teachers of nature, Luther explains the building of a woman from Adam's rib as an equal creature, albeit notably different in her sex, that, as God's image has a special vocation to rule the household and to be the nest for her husband. God created two equal beings with different sexes, Luther asserts. Even more so, God created a woman with her body to serve as the host for the revelation of the Gospel.

In this context, it is essential to note that Luther never advances the Eve-Mary typology, developed by Justin the Martyr as a parallel to the Adam-Christ typology hugely popular in the Middle Ages. According to this typology, Eve was the mother of evil and death, the devil's gateway, while Mary was the antithesis of that. On the other hand, whereas many sixteenth-century reformers, such as John Calvin, dismissed the figure of Mary for removing focus from the central Christian message, Luther never questions the Mary of orthodox tradition. He remains faithful to upholding Mary as the sinless virgin mother of God, but adds his own bent: Mary is a real, natural woman who gave birth to Christ without a man, commending her femininity rather than her virginity.[23] She is a natural woman (*weiber*) and mother of the child of humanity (*Menschenkind*) as Luther would comment on Galatians 4:4.

---

[23] Luther, WA 10/I, 352–369.

In his exposition of *Magnificat* (Luke 1:46–56), addressed to his supporter Prince John Frederick, as a *Fürstenspiegel*, Luther employs Mary as the epitome of humanity. Through Mary, he demonstrates that imperial powers and the demonic are unmasked and the human humanised in the lowly maiden. What makes the human Mary special is the fact that God took on human flesh in and through her. Explicating the depth and reality of Mary's poverty, disgrace and lowliness, Luther presents *Magnificat* as a model of God's just ruling from which the Prince should learn. The example of Mary shows that God chooses the low and despised, not any form of special piety or humility and as some deed that frees people of sin and perdition in the sight of God.[24] Luther thus presents her – *sola scriptura* – as someone ordinary: "a poor and plain citizen's daughter".[25] Precisely because she is an ordinary woman, Mary possesses the human characteristics that enable her to experience divine grace and justice and to bear Christ. Once again, the radical incarnation theology is the motor of the Reformer's teaching.

In his portrayal of Sarah, Abraham's wife, Luther draws significantly on patristic exegesis. Like his forebears, but distinct from Calvin and Zwingli, Luther goes at great length to defend Sarah for her sin of laughing when God promised her a son (Gen 18) because of her importance in the history of salvation. He excuses her due to her being

---

[24] Luther, WA 7, 538–604.
[25] Luther, WA 7, 548.

beyond the age of childbearing, and due to her and Abraham's being chaste in their relationship. Luther displays this same generosity towards Rachel and Leah (Gen 29-30), Rebecca (Gen 24 and 27), and the wife of Lot (Gen 19), perceiving them as heroic women who overcome their own shortcomings. They are repentant sinners, faithful women that played an important role in the events in the history of salvation.[26]

In the same manner, in his exegesis of women in the New Testament Luther attributes them with the function of faithful disciples. He discards the medieval allegorical interpretations of such figures as Mary and Martha or of Mary Magdalene. To Luther, the story of Mary and Martha is not an allegory of the contemplative and active life; it is rather about real women and the importance of faith over works. Concurrently, Luther delivers a unique interpretation of Luke 7:36-50 in his sermon on *Two Kinds of Righteousness* (1519).[27] Departing from traditional portrayals of Mary Magdalene as a sinful "woman of the city", Luther highlights her as paradigmatically righteous. This is an aesthetic, narrative strategy that is connected to the reality he faced and wanted to change. He envisioned removing prostitution as an industry (no longer accepted by the church institution) and imagined including ordinary women as valuable partners in the

---

[26] See Luther's comments on these various chapters in Genesis, WA 42-43.
[27] Luther, WA 2, 145-152.

community. Hence, female figures from the Bible are generally depicted as those who by way of their heroic self-humiliation conform to Christ's kenotic self-debasement (Phil 2:6–11) and consequently are exalted as true disciples of Christ. Like Sara, Lea, Mary and Martha, Mary the mother of Christ, and the woman who had been menstruating for twelve years – Mary Magdalene represents the faithfulness that can overcome social debasement as well as other worldly tribulations because they are concerned about the other, serving the fellow human being without concern for themselves: "Mary is nothing but righteous",[28] Luther asserts. These female figures are beacons of how justification through faith works, and are thus also role models for powerful males, such as Simon the Leper or Prince John Frederick, on how to act or rule.

5. *Gender and Church*

Luther's view of gender and church must be perceived within the framework of his entire theology and closely related to his transformation of ecclesiology and ministry *in toto*. His doctrines on justification and ecclesiology

---

[28] Luther, *Sermon on the Two Kinds of Righteousness*, translation, introduction, and annotations by E.M. Wiberg Pedersen, in *Word and faith* (vol. 2 of *The Annotated Luther*, Minneapolis, Minn.: Fortress Press, 2015) 21. Cf. Karant-Nunn/Wiesner-Hanks, *Luther on Women*.

are built on the theological conviction that all human beings, women and men of faith, are equal. Everything else would contradict the substance of his Reformation theology. This becomes clear in the texts where he explicates his idea of the priesthood of all believers in opposition to the papal understanding of priesthood as something very special, qualitatively and ontologically different from other human beings. In his 1523 treatise on the institution of church ministry, Luther explains how, following 1 Peter 2:5, all those baptised are priests, and as their priestly rights and obligations each one has

> to teach, preach and proclaim the word of God, baptise, consecrate and administer the Lord's supper, bind and solve from sins, pray for others, sacrifice oneself and judge all teachers and spirits.[29]

Yet, as has already been stated, Christ chose all Christians for this ministry:

> Christ has subjected you and all that is yours, all out of divine power, he has given all the authority and power to assess and judge, to read and preach [...] Those who are blessed by God are all pious and true Christians.[30]

---

[29] Luther, *De instituendis ministris ecclesiae*, WA 12, 180. Cf. *De Captivitate Babylonica ecclesiae praeludium*, WA 6, 484–573.
[30] Luther, *Vom Missbrauch der Messe*, WA 8, 496.

These are rather powerful statements: all Christians, men and women, have the same right and obligation to teach, preach and consecrate. All Christians have the same divine power to judge, read and preach, further confirmed in a letter to Spalatin, when Luther – with reference to 1 Peter 2:10 – asserts that: "The apostle Peter drives me strongly when he says that we are all priests (*sacerdotes*)".[31] The Reformer concludes that all are equal in the ministry of the word and sacrament as well as in human status.

Two important aspects of Luther's idea of the priesthood stand out: it is a responsibility towards one's neighbour, has a socialising function and there is but one ministry, not a *munus triplex*. Luther's texts propound the equality of believers in Christ through baptism, also pertaining to ministry:

> Let us thus be steadfast and let anyone who acknowledges to be a Christian know that we are equally priests, that is, we have the same right pertaining to word and sacrament. However, it is true that this right can only be used by someone according to the consensus of the community or better according to its call (for what is common to all, no single person can use it unless called). If ordination is anything at all, it is no more than a ritual by which a person is called to an ecclesial ministry. The priesthood [*sacerdotium*] in itself is nothing but the ministry of the word [*ministerium verbi*], and the word

---

[31] Luther, *Luther an Spalatin*, WA, BR 1, 595.

> of the gospel, indeed, not that of the law. Diakonia is a ministry – not for reading bible texts as is the use today – but for the task of distributing the means of the church to the poor.[32]

As in his treatise *On the Freedom of a Christian*, Luther makes a significant differentiation within the priesthood of all believers.[33] The difference lies in the calling. While everyone is spiritually and equally called as a priest through baptism and faith in Christ, only some are called to the ministry of the word (*ministerium verbi*).

Furthermore, Luther's definition of the ministry of the word is quite revolutionary. Not only does he see baptism as the true ordination, but he also rejects and dissolves the ontological difference between lay person and priest as claimed by the papal church:

> Scripture thus teaches us that what we call priesthood is a ministry. Therefore, I do not see why the person who has become priest should not again be able to become lay as lay and priest only differ pertaining to ministry.[34]

As a logical result, Luther denounces a sacramental understanding of ordination, hence also denouncing that the ordained priest should have received a special and

---

[32] Luther, *On the Babylonian Captivity of the Church*, WA 6, 566.
[33] Luther, *De libertate christiana,* WA 7, 20–28.
[34] Luther, WA 6, 567.

indelible character (*character indelebilis*). Again, he argues from Scripture: in no place in Scripture is there the slightest mention of a sacramental ordination of priests or of a special indelibly holy character given to a priest or bishop, or even the pope, in ordination that should provide them with a particular holiness such that only they can approach and touch the altar. Luther points to the absurdity of such an understanding of a qualitative and ontological division between priest and lay person. Not only is it without scriptural basis, but it displays rather a total ignorance of Christ and what it is to be a Christian, the Reformer asserts.

> Any Christian is, indeed, anointed by the oil of the Holy Spirit and sanctified on body and soul, and in the old church anyone received the Eucharist with their hands in the same way as priests today touch the bread and the chalice. It is but superstition that nowadays puffs it up as a big thing if a layperson touches the chalice itself or the cloth going with it. Not even nuns, holy virgins, are permitted to wash the altar cloth. Look, for God's sake, how much this ordination's sacrosanct sacredness has proliferated! I expect that in the future laypersons will be allowed to touch the altar only when they offer money. On my part I'm about to explode when I think of these most horrific people's impious tyranny, when I think of how they deceive and destroy the liberty and glory of Christian faith by way of such childish tricks.[35]

[35] Luther, WA 6, 566.

Luther ridicules the fact that the established church does not regard even nuns holy enough to approach the altar.

The next revolutionary move Luther makes pertaining to ministry is to transpose the power of the pope to Scripture itself: the substance of ministry does not lie in the power (*potestas*) of a selected elite but in the word, in the Gospel, given to all believers, which he also does when he clearly sees the situation of the church as one of emergency. His comment on the papal church is that "Paul raised women over men as prophets, and that in 1 Corinthians 11 he taught women to pray and prophesy [...] Thus, order rather calls for nurture [*zucht*] and that women are silent when men speak. However when no man preaches, it is necessary that women preach".[36] Merely by stating that women can preach in emergency situations, Luther is revolutionary, if considered in the historical context.

A few years later, however, Luther seems to withdraw some of his more radical views on ministry. Holsten Fagerberg has pointed out that in fact Luther never wrote a systematic doctrine on ministry but mostly formulated his view on ministry in his polemical texts. This is true of almost all Luther's theology, though I would maintain that a certain nucleus pertaining to the doctrine of justification and its relevance for the understanding of ministry as a non-hierarchical ministry of the word is consistent. Hence, Luther changed some aspects in his view on ministry after 1525 when his strife with the spiritual movements,

---

[36] Ibid.

the 'enthusiasts', peaked.[37] To avoid their spiritual understanding of the ministry as an inner calling, he began again to focus more on an ordination in tandem with the outward calling. Simultaneously, he seems to have started claiming a difference between women and men regarding the special priesthood, though never regarding the priesthood of all believers. These are, however, very rare statements, probably because the question was not at the core of his theology. So far, I have found only two texts where Luther, while maintaining the priesthood of all believers, claims that women can teach and console and thus prophesy, but not preach in public. But in neither text does Luther forbid women to preach, and in neither text does he give a solid or consistent argument for women not to preach. Quite the contrary: he goes far towards including women in the ministry.

The first text in question is Luther's sermon on Joel 2:28 (1531). Luther here finds evidence for the need of a new priesthood, one that is not dependent on the person and the person's status. Having stated that the four daughters of Philip (Luke) were prophetesses, however, he surmises:

> A woman can do this. Not preach in public, but console people and teach. A woman can do this just as much as a man. There are certainly women and girls who are able to comfort others and teach true words, that is, who can

---

[37] H. Fagerberg, "Amt, Reformationszeit", in vol. 2 of *Theologische Realencyclopädie* (36 vol., Berlin/New York: De Gruyter, 1978).

> explain Scripture and teach or console other people so that they will be well. This all counts as prophesying, not preaching. In the same way, a mother should teach her children and family, because she has been given the true words of the Holy Spirit and understands [...].[38]

Luther's message may seem inordinately conservative and self-contradictory. Yet, here again, we should understand it in its immediate context of Catholic theology that lent no authority to women whatsoever. The novelty of his doctrine on ministry becomes particularly evident when Luther continues by restating the major point that all types of people without discrimination are included in the new priesthood, regardless of sex and status: "Scripture says that a woman is not a woman, a man not a man. In Christ, Caiaphas the esteemed man is no better than a toll collector. A Carthusian who has been forty years in his order is no better than a maid who carries grass for the cows".[39]

We find the second reference to the matter in 1532, in his direct opposition to the Anabaptists and their claim to an inner, spiritual calling to speak when they feel like it during the service. Against such disorderly conduct that disturbs the actual preaching of the word, Luther is adamant: according to Paul, not just anyone can grasp the word. Whereas Joel held that everyone, men and women,

---

[38] Luther, WA 34, 482.
[39] Luther WA 34, 485.

could prophesy, the Holy Spirit through Paul has commanded that women should be silent (1 Cor 14:34), even though Paul knows the words of Joel:

> In the congregation or in the churches where there is a ministry of preaching, they should be silent and not preach. Otherwise, they may pray, sing, say praise and amen; at home, they may read and teach one another, admonish, console, and interpret Scripture as best they can.[40]

Interestingly, Luther actually wonders why the spiritualists and enthusiasts do not promote women's power and influence more by referring to Old Testament female figures that were both prophets and worldly rulers. Luther is concerned that the proper order and the right vocation, first and foremost preaching, are the most important task of the church for him.[41] As he states, these women's ministry was not compelled by their own pious urge and without any (outer) calling.

---

[40] Luther WA 30, 524.

[41] At the basis of these questions, there would be the question of the proper education. It should be noticed that, just as the Catholic Church did not offer the same high education to girls/women as it did to boys/men, neither did secular regimes allow women to receive the university education that the ministry of preaching required in Lutheran churches. For example, in Denmark, the study of theology was not open to women until 1904, after other university studies were slowly being opened to women, with medicine being the first in 1875.

However, in *On Councils and the Church* of 1539 Luther goes back to his 1521 teaching that all people are equally priests. Luther lists seven marks of the church (the word of God, baptism, Eucharist, absolution, ministry, prayer, and the cross) that all belong to the entire Christian people, the people of God. He further emphasises that receiving the Eucharist, turned by the Catholic Church into an exclusive sacrament for those particularly holy, is totally inclusive, whether the recipient be priest or lay person, whether man or woman. When describing the ministry of the word as the fifth of his seven marks (*notae ecclesiae*), Luther releases it from an ontological sacredness of the priest, perceiving it as a central function of, and for, the congregation. The task of preaching, he asserts – not the person effecting the task – is the issue.[42] Hence, the word of God and the sacraments are not dependent on who pronounces them but must be proclaimed orally by "people like you and me",[43] that is, open to every Christian. Yet, in what looks like a parenthesis, Luther exempts women (and children) from this principle of the task, the person doing the task of preaching not being the issue. Luther does not say that women are not allowed to be ministers, he merely exempts them, only to open the task of preaching to women immediately afterwards: they are called to preach in situations of need.[44] Furthermore, Luther makes

---

[42] Luther, WA 50, 633.
[43] Luther, WA 50, 629.
[44] Luther, WA 50, 633.

a bold move when he continues by measuring the knowledge of the papal high offices with that of a schoolchild. However highly the papal hierarchy regards itself, a seven-year-old girl will know more with regard to the Gospel and Christian doctrine, he (who loved all six of his children, three of whom daughters) ironically claims.[45]

Luther continues to see the pastoral office as divinely instituted, but according to his incarnational theology, this also means humanising it.[46] No pastor is more than a human being and no less a sinner than any member of the community of calling. Whereas the Catholic understanding of ministry is based on an ordination tied to a hierarchy of especially sacral males (*officium sacerdos*), Luther's understanding of ministry is based on baptism, the true sacrament of ordination, tied to Christ and subsequently to the equality of all baptised believers. The minister is a follower (*successor*) of the Gospel and as such a servant of the word (*ministerium verbi*). Whereas the Catholic *vicarius Christi* is a substitute of Christ's divine nature, the Lutheran *ministerium verbi* is a representation of the incarnate Christ, the in-fleshed Logos. With his incarnational understanding of God, Luther's point is that God wants first and foremost to be known as a human being, spelt out in his oeuvre, for example in *On the Freedom*, as Christ's

---

[45] Ibid.
[46] Luther, *In epistolam S Pauli ad Galatas Commentarius*, WA 40/I, 59, here commenting on Galatians 1:1 thus: "Ministri sunt ex nobis electi [...] Deus vocat nos omnes ad ministerium vocatione per hominem estque divina vocatio".

similitudo hominis, his likeness to a human being. Accordingly, he never determines Christ as a male but always as a human (*homo* or *Mensch*) (cf. Luther on translation). Likewise, when Luther propounds his central theological principles, he normally employs the generic term human being (*homo* or *Mensch*), not the gender term male (*vir* or *Mann*).

While establishment's interpretation of 1 Corinthians 11:7 and 14:34 was radically literal, so that Canon law justified the cultic impediment of human femaleness by women's lack of creational *imago Dei*,[47] Luther never quotes the texts verbatim. Thomas Aquinas, Bonaventura and Duns Scotus each in their own way argued that men alone can be ordained since women, due to their created state of subjection, are unable to signify Christ's male eminence and authority. Luther never recurs to such arguments as female subjection or Christ's maleness pertaining to the church ministry. In fact, he was predominantly gender-neutral when dealing with the church ministry, and we only find a few instances of ultra-brief formulations regarding women and ministry, as demonstrated here. If we study Luther's treatment of 1 Corinthians 14:34, we find his exposition neither adamantly insistent (except perhaps in the case of the Anabaptists and their speaking in tongues) nor consistent. If we read the Reformer with

---

[47] K.E. Børresen, "Impedimentum Sexus: The Cultic Impediment of Female Humanity", in A.H. Grung/M.B. Kartzow/A.C. Solevåg (ed.), *Bodies, Borders, Believers: Ancient Texts and Present Conversations* (Eugene, Oregon: Pickwick Publications 2014) 7.

all the nuances and inconsistencies – even inner self-contradictions, the dominant question is whether Luther was simply as ambivalent as the tradition before him and the peers of his time. If one says, as I do, that he was not as ambivalent as most of his contemporaries but rather more positive towards women – could we then take the inconsistencies to be intentional ambiguity? Could it be that Luther left the question open because it was too dangerous to elaborate fully, as his condemnation by pope and emperor in 1520–1521 showed, as did the fate of nuns, such as Isabel de la Cruz, who was accused of offending the authority of the Church in 1524, and severely punished by the auto-da-fé in 1529?[48] I propose that in his endeavours for reform Luther was caught between his own ideas of freedom and a highly hierarchical and patriarchal society and church.

6. *Concluding Remarks*

Many women were for good reasons captivated by Luther's theology, with its humanisation of the ecclesial office concomitant with its sacralisation of the ordinary human life, and acted upon it. The way sixteenth-century society was regulated, however, opposed severe resistance to them, and with the consolidation of the Reform churches in the

---

[48] A. Weber, *Teresa of Avila and the Rethoric of Feminity* (Princeton: Princeton University Press, 1990), 27.

generations following Luther, such resistance only grew until it was finally broken with new societal ideas and new views of gender during the nineteenth and twentieth centuries. This did not happen in spite of Luther's theology but because of it. Luther's neutral gender language when speaking in principle of ministry, together with the gaps that his creative ambiguity left open to interpretation, led to the admittance of women's ordination, first in Denmark from 1947, and from then on gradually being extended to most Lutheran Churches.

Whereas most Lutheran Churches now have a gender neutral priesthood, gender-specific male priesthood is preserved in canon 1024 of *Codex Iuris Canonici* (1983), which according to Kari Børresen literally repeats canon 968, §1 of the 1917 version: "Sacram ordinationem valide recipit solus vir baptizatus (only a baptised male can receive valid ordination)". The issue is still so divisive that it had to be excluded from the *Lutheran-Roman Catholic Commision on Unity* (1995–2006) if the LWF were to be able to pursue its ecumenical dialogue with the Pontifical Council for Promoting Christian Unity.[49]

---

[49] Børresen, "Impedimentum Sexus", 2–3.

Notes on Contributors

Saverio Campanini is an Italian professor of Jewish Language and Literature at the University of Bologna. Previously, he was visiting professor at the Department of studies of Asian and Mediterran Africa at the Ca' Foscari University of Venice. He was also director of research at the Institut de Recherche et d'Histoires des Textes in Paris and lecturer at the Ecole Pratique des Hautes Etudes at the Sorbonne. His research focuses on three main themes: Christian Kabbalah in the Renaissance, Hebrew manuscripts and the history of Jewish studies. He is editorial consultant for publishing houses such as Adelphi and Brill, and for the editors of several academic journals such as *Journal of Jewish Studies, Jewish Studies Quarterly, Sefarad, Kabbalah, Revue des Études Juives, Materia Giudaica, Zutot. Perspectives on Jewish Culture, Henoch, Renaissance Studies, La Bibliofilia, Journal of Transcultural Medieval Studies, Allgemeine Zeitschrift für Philosophie*. His latest publications are "Carteggio d'autunno tedesco. Uno scambio di lettere tra Gershom Scholem e Nicolaus Sombart a proposito di Carl Schmitt e d'altro", in *Schifanoia* (52-53, 2017, 41-62) and "Elchana Hebraeorum doctor et cabalista". Le avventure di un libro e dei suoi lettori", in *Umanesimo e cultura ebraica nel Rinascimento italiano* (Firenze: Angelo Pontecorboli Editore, 2016, 90–114).

Pierre Gisel is a Swiss Protestant theologian of the Reformed Church; he is one of the most prominent francophone theologians in the world of modern theology, playing a considerable role in the contemporary mutations in the disciplines concerning theology and religious sciences. In addition to his many experiences as a visiting professor at European universities (Paris, Freiburg), Pierre Gisel was a visiting professor at the Faculty of Theology at the University of Quebec. He is also a professor and dean of the Faculty of Theology and Religious Sciences at the University of Lausanne in Switzerland. His research has focused on three main themes: the role of theology in the humanities, the reflection on monotheistic religions and the relationship between theology and religious sciences. He has published over forty books, his latest works being *L'humain entre résistance et dépassement. Entretiens sur le christianisme et le religieux en société contemporaine*, co-authored with Michèle Bolli-Voélin (Le-Mont-sur-Lousanne: Ouverture, 2017) and *Qu'est-ce qu'une tradition? Ce dont elle répond, son usage, sa pertinence* (Paris: Hermann, 2017).

Enzo Pace is full professor of Sociology and the Sociology of Religion at the University of Padova in Italy and visiting professor at the École des Hautes Études en Sciences Sociales in Paris. He was formerly President of the International Society for the Sociology of Religion (ISSR/SISR). He is co-editor of the *Annual Review of the Sociology of Religion* (Brill), and a member of several Editorial Committees. In particular, he works for: *Religioni & Società* at University of Firenze, *Religiologiques* at Montreal University, *Horizontes Anthropologicos* at the Federal University of Rio Grande do Sul in Brazil, and *International Journal of Latin American Religions* in Santiago do Chile. His recent publications are: *Religious Diversity in a Pluralistic Society*, in *Religions* (17, 2018); *Cristianesimo extra-large* (Bologna: Dehoniane, 2018) and "Les cyber-religions entre dématérialisation du sacré et réenchantement du monde" in *Sociétés,* (138/1, 2018).

Risto Saarinen received his doctorate in Theology in 1988 and his doctorate in Philosophy in 1994. He was awarded the chair of professor of Ecumenics at the University of Helsinki in 2001 and in 2014 became Director of the Reason and Religious Recognition Centre of Excellence at the Academy of Finland; he will hold this post until 2019. In 1994–1999, he was professor at the Institute for Ecumenical Research in Strasbourg. From 2005 to 2010, he was visiting professor at the Universities of Aarhus and, from 2011 to 2014, visiting professor at KU Leuven. Risto was appointed a member of Academia Europaea in 2015 and was awarded an honorary doctorate in Theology at the University of Copenhagen in 2017. His recent publications include *Recognition and Religion: A Historical and Sysrtematic Study* ((Oxford: Oxford University Press, 2016) and *Luther and the Gift* (Tübingen: Mohr Siebeck, 2017).

Heinz Schilling is one of the most distinguished historians of the Early Modern Era. The main themes of his research concern: European comparative history, Reformation and European confessionalisation, immigration and minorities in early Europe, political theory in early modern Europe. In 1992, he was appointed to the newly established chair of Early Modern European History as part of the foundation of the Institute of Historical Studies (Instituts für Geschichtswissenschaften) at the Humboldt University in Berlin, which he held until his retirement at the end of 2010. In 2009, he was awarded an honorary doctorate in Theology (Gottingen) and, in 2014, in History (Trento). His most recent publications are *1517: Weltgeschichte eines Jahres* (Munich: C.H. Beck, 2017) and *Martin Luther, Rebell in einer Zeit des Umbruchs. Eine Biographie* (C.H. Beck, 2012).

Perry Schmidt-Leukel is professor of Religious Studies and Intercultural Theology at the University of Münster in Germany and Director of the Institute for Religious Studies and Inter-Faith Theology. He is one of the principal investigators in the Cluster of Excellence Religion and Politics at the University of Münster. He previously taught at the Universities of Munich, Innsbruck, Salzburg and Glasgow. Schmidt-Leukel is internationally renowned as one of the leading proponents of a pluralist theology of religions. His main research interests are in the fields of inter-faith relations, Buddhist-Christian dialogue, theologies of religions in the various religious traditions and inter-faith theology. In 2015 Schmidt-Leukel was the first German to present the prestigious Gifford-Lectures in 25 years. He has published *Religious Pluralism and Interreligious Theology. The Gifford Lectures – An Extended Edition* (Manyknoll, N.Y.: Orbis Books, 2017) and *Buddhist and Christian Attitudes to Religious Diversity*, co-edited with Hans-Peter Grosshans and Samuel Ngun Ling (Yangon: Ling's Family Publications, 2017).

Lieve Teugels received her doctorate in Theology at the KU Leuven in Belgium in 1994. She specialised in the Hebrew Bible and rabbinic literature, especially midrash. From 1994 to 2002, she was assistant professor of Judaism at the Faculty of Theology at Utrecht University. In 2000–2002, she was visiting scholar at the Jewish Theological Seminary of America in New York. She lived in the US until 2009. Lieve was appointed part-time assistant professor of Semitics and Jewish Studies at the PThU in Amsterdam in June 2016. She is furthermore involved in the NWO project

Notes on Contributors

Parables and the Partings of the Ways at Utrecht University, in which she works on an annotated critical edition of early Jewish parables. Lieve is the author of two books *Aggadat Bereshit. Translated from the Hebrew with an Introduction and Notes* (Leiden/Boston/Köln: Brill, 2001) and *Bible and Midrash. The Story of 'The Wooing of Rebekah'(Gen 24)* (Leuven/Paris/Dudley, Mass: Peeters, 2004).

Else Marie Wiberg Pedersen is associate professor in Systematic Theology, with special responsibility for Dogmatics, at Aarhus University, Denmark. She specialises in medieval and Reformation theology from a gender perspective, but also engages in contemporary theology with a focus on ecclesiology and ministry. She has published widely on Bernard of Clairvaux and Martin Luther and at present heads an international project on Luther from the subalterns from which a book will emerge in 2019. Furthermore, she is currently working on an English translation of her Danish monograph *Bernhard of Clairvaux. Teolog eller mystiker?* (Bernard of Clairvaux. A Theologian or a Mystic?) to be published by Brepols.

Names Index

A
Abraham 29, 204-205
Abulafia, Abraham 29-30
Achilles 76, 84
Adam 36, 200-203
Adams, Jonathan 36
Adriani, Matthaeus 36-38, 40
Agamben, Giorgio 57
Albera, Dionigi 72-73
Alberigo, Giuseppe 11
Alberts, Hildegard 33
Alexander VI (Roderic Llançol de Borja), Pope 141
Allievi, Stefano 78
Amman, Caspar 38
Anshelm, Thomas 33, 37
Arcangelo da Borgonovo 20, 43
Aristotle 90, 93, 201
Augustine 54, 94, 100-101, 122, 195, 200
Augustine of Hippo 100

B
Bacon, Roger 25
Bainton, Roland 192
Balaam 30
Barth, Karl 108-109, 115
Baubérot, Jean 83
Bede the Venerable 25
Berding, Helmut 133
Berger, Peter 81
Bernard of Clairvaux 96, 102, 197, 227-228
Bernini, G. Lorenzo 144
Bertolani, Barbara 77
Bhikkhu Buddhadāsa 168, 171
Birmelé, André 114
Blamires, Alcuin 200
Bloch, Renée 180
Böchenförde, Ernst-Wolfgang 85
Bodin, Jean 143
Boitani, Piero 90, 92
Børresen, Kari E. 217, 219
Boyarin, Daniel 183
Bréchon, Pierre 81
Bromiley, Geoffrey W. 108
Buchwald, Reinhard 194
Bultmann, Rudolf 107-109, 115
Burckhardt, Titus 153
Burgio, Giuseppe 73
Busi, Giulio 26, 35

C
Cadeddu, Francesca 3-5, 7
Calvin, John 98-101, 103, 135, 203-204
Campanini, Saverio 5, 12, 15, 27, 29, 30, 33, 35, 38, 40, 42, 46, 221
Campos, Fabiano V. 49
Canisius, Peter 140
Carracci, Ludovico 187, 189
Carretto, Lodovico (ha-Kohen, Todros) 44-45
Casanova, José 81
Chalamet, Christophe 49
Charles V, Emperor 142, 194
Châtellier, Louis 141
Ching, Julia 160
Cicero 53-54

Classen, Albrecht 193
Coakley, Sarah 192
Cobb, John 168-169, 171
Comte-Sponville, André 56
Copenhaver, Brian P. 31
Corazzol, Giacomo 29
Cornille, Catherine 164

D
Dall'Asta, Matthias 35
de Almeida, Tatiane A. 49
Denti, Domenica 77
Denzinger, Heinrich 194
Detienne, Marcel 58
Dörner, Gerald 35
Drew, Rose 166
Drusius, Johannes 26
Dürer, Albrecht 136
Dworkin, Ronald 56

E
Eade, John 73
Ehrenfreund, Jacques 55, 63, 68
El'azar of Worms 28
Eliade, Mircea 169
Elijah, the Prophet 34, 189
Epstein, Jacob N. 181
Erasmus 46
Evagrius Ponticus 31

F
Fagerberg, Holsten 211-212
Farmer, Stephen A. 21, 23-24
Ferrari, Mauro 3, 77
Ferry, Luc 56
Fichte, Johann G. 88
Ficino, Marsilio 19, 101
Flavius Mithridates (Bulfarağ Shemu'el ben Nissim, Guglielmo Raimondo Moncada) 23, 27
Ford, James 163
Forst, Rainer 89
Foucault, Michel 57, 69
Fowler, James 166
Fraenkel, Yonah 183
Franck, Sebastian 200-201
Freud, Sigmund 50
Fries, Heinrich 114-115
Furseth, Inger 74

G
Gauchet, Marcel 50
Giotto 25-26
Gisel, Pierre 5, 12, 49, 55, 63, 68, 222
Goethe, J. Wolfgang 122, 173
Göle, Nilüfer 81
Gramsci, Antonio 51
Griffin, David R. 168
Grung, Anne H. 217

H
Habermas, Jürgen 82, 86
Hegel, Georg W.F. 88-91, 103, 110, 119-120
Heiler, Friedrich 160
Heim, S. Mark 168, 170-171
Helaas, Paul 81
Heller, Dagmar 91
Hénaff, Marcel 90
Heredia, Pablo de 30
Heß, Cordelia 36
Hietamäki, Minna 91
Hoffmann, Veronika 90
Hokusai, Katsushika 150-151
Holenstein, Elmar 157-159

Names Index

Honneth, Axel 88-91, 97, 109, 111
Hosea 37
Hutchison, John A. 169

I
Ibn Waqar, Joseph 23
Idel, Moshe 23
Iesua (Yehoshua) 25
IHSUH 32-34, 36, 44
Isidore of Sevilla 16, 25
Izutsu, Toshihiko 176

J
Jackson, William J. 153
Jäger, Willigis 80
James, William 163, 165-166
Jellinek, Georg 120
Jerome 25, 41
Jesus 15-16, 18-21, 23-40, 43, 45-47, 93, 112, 129, 154, 175-177, 188-189
Jesus ben Sira 33
Jesus the Nazarene 37
Jesus (Yeshu, Yeshush) 5, 15, 16, 18-21, 23-40, 43, 45-47, 93, 112, 129, 154, 175-177, 188-189
John à Lasco 135
Joshua 33, 36-37
Julius II (Giuliano della Rovere), Pope 141
Jüngel, Eberhard 109

K
Kak, Subhash 154
Kant, Immanuel 104
Karant-Nunn, Susan 200-201, 206

Kartzow, Marianne B. 217
Kasper, Walter 114-115
Kaufmann, Thomas 118, 133
Kittel, Gerhard 107
Klaus, Peter 201
Krebs, Manfred 33
Küng, Hans 160

L
Lactantius 54
Laurens, Pierre 101
Leah (Rachel's sister) 205
Lelli, Fabrizio 23, 42
Leo X (Giovanni de' Medici), Pope 141
Lim, Timothy T.N. 90
Lot 205
Luke, the Evangelist 188, 204-205, 212
Luther, Martin 6, 101-102, 117, 119-142, 144-145, 191-219, 224-225, 227

M
Mall, Ram Adhar 156-157
Mancini, Silvia 55, 68
Mandelbrot, Benoît 148-150, 153, 161
Martha 205-206
Marx, Karl 50
Mary 96, 132, 193, 197, 203-206
Mary Magdalene 96, 205-206
McNeill, John T. 99
Melamed, Ezra Z. 181
Melloni, Alberto 7, 49
Mendelsohn, Moses 179-180
Michelangelo 26
Miller, Clarence H. 46
Moedas, Carlos 8

231

More, Thomas 46, 64, 123
Mortensen, Viggo 170
Moses 6, 33, 37, 179, 180-186, 188-189, 202
Moses Maimonides 179-180
Müller, Max 173-174

N
Nakamura, Hajime 156
Natali, Cristiana 73
Nehring, Andreas 167
Nicolaus of Cues 31
Nicolaus of Lyra 31
Niculescu, Mira 166
Nietzsche, Friedrich W. 50
Nydhal, Hannah 79
Nydhal, Ole 79

O
Obadia, Lionel 79
Otto, Rudolph 165
Ozment, Steve 192

P
Pace, Enzo 5, 12, 71, 73-74, 77, 202, 223
Paul of Burgos 31
Paul, the Apostle 31, 41, 89, 93, 100, 103, 156, 195, 197, 211, 213-214
Perani, Mauro 27, 29-30
Perocco, Fabio 77
Pettersson, Per 74
Pfefferkorn, Johannes 36
Philip, the Apostle 15, 212
Pico della Mirandola, Giovanni 18, 19, 20, 22, 23, 29, 30, 37, 42, 44
Plessner, Helmut 128

Poincaré, Henri 161, 166
Poorthuis, Marcel 179
Prudentius 15

R
Rachel 205
Ratzinger, Joseph (Benedict XVI, Pope) 86, 114-115
Raziel 36
Rebecca 205
Rehm, Bernhard 93
Reuchlin, Johannes 17, 20, 31, 32-39, 44-45
Rhein, Stefan 35
Ricoeur, Paul 89-90, 100-101, 103
Roper, Lyndal 192-193
Rosati, Massimo 82
Rousseau, Jean-Jacques 103
Ruparell, Tinu 164

S
Saarinen, Risto 5, 12, 87, 92, 95, 98, 100, 101-103, 107, 112, 114, 116, 224
Sarah (Abraham's wife) 192, 204
Schäfer, Peter 33
Scharffenorth, Gerta 193
Schilling, Heinz 6, 12, 117, 137, 224
Schleiermacher, Friedrich D.E. 106-107, 115
Schmidt-Leukel, Perry 6, 12, 147, 167, 225-226
Schomerus, Hilko W. 162, 163
Schönmetzer, Adolf 194
Schubert, Anselm 133
Scotus, J. Duns 217

Names Index

Secret, François 28, 31, 42
Senra, Flávio A. 49
Settle, Tanya A. 193
Shah-Kazemi, Reza 176
Shaw, Rosalind 164
Sheid, John 58
Shilo 40
Simlai 186
Simon the Leper 206
Sixtus V (Felice Peretti), Pope 143
Sloterdijk, Peter 56, 59
Solevåg, Anna R. 217
Spalding, Johann J. 104-105, 115
Stemberger, Günter 30, 185-186, 188
Stern, David 183
Stewart, Charles 164
Stjerna, Kirsi 192
Stoecker, Adolf 133
Stolz, Jörg 81
Strecker, Georg 93
Strehler, Giorgio 145
Streicher, Julius 129

T

Taylor, Charles 56, 87-91, 111
Teugels, Lieve M. 6, 12, 179, 181, 183, 226
Thomas Aquinas 54, 96, 98-99, 217
Thompson, Simon 88, 172
Thönissen, Wolfgang 114
Thraede, Klaus 193

U

Ubertini, Francesco 10

V

van der Veer, Peter 164
Vernant, Jean-Pierre 58
Veyne, Paul 57
Vilaça, Helena 74
von Bora, Katharina 198-199
von Harnack, Adolf 120, 173
von Ranke, Leopold 120

W

Waldenfels, Bernhard 157
Wallmann, Johannes 132
Wandrey, Irene 33
Weber, Alison 120, 218
Weber, Max 120, 218
Wénin, André 183
Westhelle, Vitor 194
Wiberg Pedersen, Else M. 6, 12, 191, 206, 227
Wiesner-Hanks, Merry E. 191-192, 200-201, 206
Wilkinson, Robert J. 31
Winkler, Heinrich A. 128
Wirszubski, Chaim 22, 42
Woodhead, Linda 81

Y

Yeshu 25-27, 29-30, 34, 37, 40, 42
Yeshush 40

Z

Zeno of Elea 76
Zhe, Ji 80
Zorzi, Francesco (Francesco Giorgio Veneto) 38-44

233

Finito di stampare nel mese di febbraio 2019
presso Futura Grafica 70, Roma

www.ingramcontent.com/pod-product-compliance
Lightning Source LLC
Chambersburg PA
CBHW051540230426
43669CB00015B/2672